Understanding Search Engines

SOFTWARE • ENVIRONMENTS • TOOLS

The series includes handbooks and software guides as well as monographs
on practical implementation of computational methods, environments, and tools.
The focus is on making recent developments available in a practical format
to researchers and other users of these methods and tools.

Editor-in-Chief

Jack J. Dongarra
University of Tennessee and Oak Ridge National Laboratory

Editorial Board

James W. Demmel, University of California, Berkeley
Dennis Gannon, Indiana University
Eric Grosse, AT&T Bell Laboratories
Ken Kennedy, Rice University
Jorge J. Moré, Argonne National Laboratory

Software, Environments, and Tools

Michael W. Berry and Murray Browne, *Understanding Search Engines: Mathematical Modeling and Text Retrieval, Second Edition*

Craig C. Douglas, Gundolf Haase, and Ulrich Langer, *A Tutorial on Elliptic PDE Solvers and Their Parallelization*

Louis Komzsik, *The Lanczos Method: Evolution and Application*

Bard Ermentrout, *Simulating, Analyzing, and Animating Dynamical Systems: A Guide to XPPAUT for Researchers and Students*

V. A. Barker, L. S. Blackford, J. Dongarra, J. Du Croz, S. Hammarling, M. Marinova, J. Wasniewski, and P. Yalamov, *LAPACK95 Users' Guide*

Stefan Goedecker and Adolfy Hoisie, *Performance Optimization of Numerically Intensive Codes*

Zhaojun Bai, James Demmel, Jack Dongarra, Axel Ruhe, and Henk van der Vorst, *Templates for the Solution of Algebraic Eigenvalue Problems: A Practical Guide*

Lloyd N. Trefethen, *Spectral Methods in MATLAB*

E. Anderson, Z. Bai, C. Bischof, S. Blackford, J. Demmel, J. Dongarra, J. Du Croz, A. Greenbaum, S. Hammarling, A. McKenney, and D. Sorensen, *LAPACK Users' Guide, Third Edition*

Michael W. Berry and Murray Browne, *Understanding Search Engines: Mathematical Modeling and Text Retrieval*

Jack J. Dongarra, Iain S. Duff, Danny C. Sorensen, and Henk A. van der Vorst, *Numerical Linear Algebra for High-Performance Computers*

R. B. Lehoucq, D. C. Sorensen, and C. Yang, *ARPACK Users' Guide: Solution of Large-Scale Eigenvalue Problems with Implicitly Restarted Arnoldi Methods*

Randolph E. Bank, *PLTMG: A Software Package for Solving Elliptic Partial Differential Equations, Users' Guide 8.0*

L. S. Blackford, J. Choi, A. Cleary, E. D'Azevedo, J. Demmel, I. Dhillon, J. Dongarra, S. Hammarling, G. Henry, A. Petitet, K. Stanley, D. Walker, and R. C. Whaley, *ScaLAPACK Users' Guide*

Greg Astfalk, editor, *Applications on Advanced Architecture Computers*

Françoise Chaitin-Chatelin and Valérie Frayssé, *Lectures on Finite Precision Computations*

Roger W. Hockney, *The Science of Computer Benchmarking*

Richard Barrett, Michael Berry, Tony F. Chan, James Demmel, June Donato, Jack Dongarra, Victor Eijkhout, Roldan Pozo, Charles Romine, and Henk van der Vorst, *Templates for the Solution of Linear Systems: Building Blocks for Iterative Methods*

E. Anderson, Z. Bai, C. Bischof, J. Demmel, J. Dongarra, J. Du Croz, A. Greenbaum, S. Hammarling, A. McKenney, S. Ostrouchov, and D. Sorensen, *LAPACK Users' Guide, Second Edition*

Jack J. Dongarra, Iain S. Duff, Danny C. Sorensen, and Henk van der Vorst, *Solving Linear Systems on Vector and Shared Memory Computers*

J. J. Dongarra, J. R. Bunch, C. B. Moler, and G. W. Stewart, *Linpack Users' Guide*

Understanding Search Engines

Mathematical Modeling and
Text Retrieval

Second Edition

Michael W. Berry

University of Tennessee
Knoxville, Tennessee

Murray Browne

University of Tennessee
Knoxville, Tennessee

 Society for Industrial and Applied Mathematics
Philadelphia

Copyright © 2005 by the Society for Industrial and Applied Mathematics.

10 9 8 7 6 5 4 3 2 1

All rights reserved. Printed in the United States of America. No part of this book may be reproduced, stored, or transmitted in any manner without the written permission of the publisher. For information, write to the Society for Industrial and Applied Mathematics, 3600 University City Science Center, Philadelphia, PA 19104-2688.

Trademarked names may be used in this book without the inclusion of a trademark symbol. These names are used in an editorial context only; no infringement is intended.

The illustration on the front cover was originally sketched by Katie Terpstra and later redesigned on a color workstation by Eric Clarkson and David Rogers. The concept for the design came from an afternoon in which the co-authors deliberated on the meaning of "search."

Library of Congress Cataloging-in-Publication Data

Berry, Michael W.
    Understanding search engines : mathematical modeling and text retrieval / Michael W. Berry, Murray Browne.—2nd ed.
        p. cm.
    Includes bibliographical references and index.
    ISBN 0-89871-581-4 (pbk.)
        1. Web search engines. 2. Vector spaces. 3. Text processing (Computer science) I. Browne, Murray. II. Title.

    TK5105.884.B47 2005
    025.04—dc22

                                                                    2005042539

 is a registered trademark.

*To our families
(Teresa, Amanda, Rebecca,
Cynthia, and Bonnie)*

Contents

Preface to the Second Edition

Anyone who has used a web search engine with any regularity knows that there is an element of the unknown with every query. Sometimes the user will type in a *stream-of-consciousness* query, and the documents retrieved are a perfect match, while the next query can be seemingly succinct and focused, only to earn the bane of all search results — the *no documents found* response. Oftentimes the same queries can be submitted on different databases with just the opposite results. It is an experience aggravating enough to swear off doing web searches as well as swear at the developers of such systems.

However, because of the transparent nature of computer software design, there is a tendency to forget the decisions and trade-offs that are constantly made throughout the design process affecting the performance of the system. One of the main objectives of this book is to identify to the novice search engine builder, such as the senior level computer science or applied mathematics student or the information sciences graduate student specializing in retrieval systems, the impact of certain decisions that are made at various junctures of this development. One of the major decisions in developing information retrieval systems is selecting and implementing the computational approaches within an integrated software environment. Applied mathematics plays a major role in search engine performance, and *Understanding Search Engines* (or *USE*) focuses on this area, bridging the gap between the fields of applied mathematics and information management, disciplines which previously have operated largely in independent domains.

But *USE* does not only fill the gap between applied mathematics and information management, it also fills a niche in the information retrieval literature. The work of William Frakes and Ricardo Baeza-Yates (eds.), *Information Retrieval Data Structures and Algorithms*, a 1992 collection of journal articles on various related topics, Gerald Kowalski's (1997) *Information Retrieval Systems: Theory and Implementation*, a broad overview of information retrieval systems, and Ricardo Baeza-Yates and Berthier Ribeiro-Neto's (1999) *Modern Information Retrieval*, a computer-science perspective of information retrieval, are all fine textbooks on the topic, but understandably they lack the gritty details of the mathematical computations needed to build more successful search engines.

With this in mind, *USE* does not provide an overview of information retrieval systems but prefers to assume the supplementary role to the above-mentioned books. Many of the ideas for *USE* were first presented and developed as part of a Data and Information Management course at the University of Tennessee's Computer Science Department, a course which won the 1997 Undergraduate Computational Engineering and Science Award sponsored by the United States Department of Energy and the Krell Institute. The course, which required student teams to build their own search engines, has provided invaluable background material in the development of *USE*.

As mentioned earlier, *USE* concentrates on the applied mathematics portion of search engines. Although not transparent to the pedestrian search engine user, mathematics plays an integral part in information retrieval systems by computing the emphasis the query terms have in their relationship to the database. This is especially true in vector space modeling, which is one of the predominant techniques used in search engine design. With vector space modeling, traditional orthogonal matrix decompositions from linear algebra can be used to encode both terms and documents in k-dimensional space.

There are other computational methods that are equally useful or valid. In fact, in this edition we have included a chapter on link-structure algorithms (an approach used by the Google search engine) which arise from both graph theory and linear algebra. However, in order to teach future developers the intricate details of a system, a single approach had to be selected. Therefore the reader can expect a fair amount of math, including explanations of algorithms and data structures and how they operate in information retrieval systems. This book will not hide the math (concentrated in Chapters 3, 4, and 7), nor will it allow itself to get bogged down in it either. A person with a nonmathematical background (such as an information scientist) can still appreciate some of the mathematical intricacies involved with building search engines without reading the more technical Chapters 3, 4, and 7.

To maintain its focus on the mathematical approach, *USE* has purposely avoided digressions into Java programming, HTML programming, and how to create a web interface. An informal conversational approach has been adopted to give the book a less intimidating tone, which is especially important considering the possible multidisciplinary backgrounds of its potential readers; however, standard math notation will be used. Boxed items throughout the book contain ancillary information, such as mathematical examples, anecdotes, and current practices, to help guide the discussion. Websites providing software (e.g., CGI scripts, text parsers, numerical software) and text corpora are provided in Chapter 9.

Acknowledgments

In addition to those who assisted with the first edition, the authors would like to gratefully acknowledge the support and encouragement of SIAM, who along with our readers encouraged us to update the original book. We appreciate the helpful comments and suggestions from Alan Wallace and Gayle Baker at Hodges Library, University of Tennessee, Scott Wells from the Department of Computer Science at the University of Tennessee, Mark Gauthier at H.W. Wilson Company, June Levy at Cinhahl Information Systems, and James Marcetich at the National Library of Medicine. Special thanks go to Amy Langville of the Department of Mathematics at North Carolina State University, who reviewed our new chapter on link structure-based algorithms. The authors would also like to thank graphic designer David Rogers, who updated the fine artwork of Katie Terpstra, who drew the original art.

Hopefully, *USE* will help future developers, whether they be students or software engineers, to lessen the aggravation encountered with the current state of search engines. It continues to be a dynamic time for search engines and the future of the Web itself, as both ultimately depend on how easily users can find the information they are looking for.

MICHAEL W. BERRY
MURRAY BROWNE

Preface to the First Edition

Anyone who has used a web search engine with any regularity knows that there is an element of the unknown with every query. Sometimes the user will type in a *stream-of-consciousness* query, and the documents retrieved are a perfect match, while the next query can be seemingly succinct and focused, only to earn the bane of all search results — the *no documents found* response. Oftentimes the same queries can be submitted on different databases with just the opposite results. It is an experience aggravating enough to make one swear off doing web searches as well as swear at the developers of such systems.

However, because of the transparent nature of computer software design, there is a tendency to forget the decisions and trade-offs that are constantly made throughout the design process affecting the performance of the system. One of the main objectives of this book is to identify to the novice search engine builder, such as the senior level computer science or applied mathematics student or the information sciences graduate student specializing in retrieval systems, the impact of certain decisions that are made at various junctures of this development. One of the major decisions in developing information retrieval systems is selecting and implementing the computational approaches within an integrated software environment. Applied mathematics plays a major role in search engine performance, and *Understanding Search Engines* (or *USE*) focuses on this area, bridging the gap between the fields of applied mathematics and information management, disciplines that previously have operated largely in independent domains.

But *USE* does not only fill the gap between applied mathematics and information management, it also fills a niche in the information retrieval literature. The work of William Frakes and Ricardo Baeza-Yates (eds.), *Information Retrieval: Data Structures & Algorithms*, a 1992 collection of journal articles on various related topics, and Gerald Kowalski's (1997) *Information Retrieval Systems: Theory and Implementation*, a broad overview of information retrieval systems, are fine textbooks on the topic, but both understandably lack the gritty details of the mathematical computations needed to build more successful search engines.

With this in mind, *USE* does not provide an overview of information retrieval systems but prefers to assume a supplementary role to the aforementioned books. Many of the ideas for *USE* were first presented and developed as part of a Data and Information Management course at the University of Tennessee's Computer Science Department, a course which won the 1997 Undergraduate Computational Engineering and Science Award sponsored by the United States Department of Energy and the Krell Institute. The course, which required student teams to build their own search engines, has provided invaluable background material in the development of *USE*.

As mentioned earlier, *USE* concentrates on the applied mathematics portion of search engines. Although not transparent to the pedestrian search engine user, mathematics plays an integral part in information retrieval systems by computing the emphasis the query terms have in their relationship to the database. This is especially true in vector space modeling, which is one of the predominant techniques used in search engine design. With vector space modeling, traditional orthogonal matrix decompositions from linear algebra can be used to encode both terms and documents in k-dimensional space.

However, that is not to say that other computational methods are not useful or valid, but in order to teach future developers the intricate details of a system, a single approach had to be selected. Therefore, the reader can expect a fair amount of math, including explanations of algorithms and data structures and how they operate in information retrieval systems. This book will not hide the math (concentrated in Chapters 3 and 4), nor will it allow itself to get bogged down in it either. A person with a nonmathematical background (such as an information scientist) can still appreciate some of the mathematical intricacies involved with building search engines without reading the more technical Chapters 3 and 4.

To maintain its focus on the mathematical approach, *USE* has purposely avoided digressions into Java programming, HTML programming, and how to create a web interface. An informal conversational approach has been adopted to give the book a less intimidating tone, which is especially important considering the possible multidisciplinary backgrounds of its potential readers; however, standard math notation will be used. Boxed items throughout the book contain ancillary information, such as mathematical examples, anecdotes, and current practices, to help guide the discussion. Websites providing software (e.g., CGI scripts, text parsers, numerical software) and text corpora are provided in Chapter 9.

Acknowledgments

The authors would like to gratefully acknowledge the support and encouragement of SIAM, the United States Department of Energy, the Krell Institute, the National Science Foundation for supporting related research, the University of Tennessee, the students of CS460/594 (fall semester 1997), and graduate assistant Luojian Chen. Special thanks go to Alan Wallace and David Penniman from the School of Information Sciences at the University of Tennessee, Padma Raghavan and Ethel Wittenberg in the Department of Computer Science at the University of Tennessee, Barbara Chen at H.W. Wilson Company, and Martha Ferrer at Elsevier Science SPD for their helpful proofreading, comments, and/or suggestions. The authors would also like to thank Katie Terpstra and Eric Clarkson for their work with the book cover artwork and design, respectively.

Hopefully, this book will help future developers, whether they be students or software engineers, to lessen the aggravation encountered with the current state of search engines. It is a critical time for search engines and the future of the Web itself, as both ultimately depend on how easily users can find the information they are looking for.

MICHAEL W. BERRY
MURRAY BROWNE

DOONESBURY ©G.B. Trudeau. Reprinted with permission of UNIVERSAL PRESS
SYNDICATE. All rights reserved.

Chapter 1

Introduction

We expect a lot from our search engines. We ask them vague questions
about topics that we are unfamiliar about ourselves and in turn anticipate a
concise, organized response. We type in *principal* when we meant *principle*.
We incorrectly type the name *Lanzcos* and fully expect the search engine to
know that we really meant *Lanczos*. Basically we are asking the computer
to supply the information we want, instead of the information we asked for.
In short, users are asking the computer to reason intuitively. It is a tall
order, and in some search systems you would probably have better success
if you laid your head on the keyboard and coaxed the computer to try to
read your mind.

Of course these problems are nothing new to the reference librarian who
works the desk at a college or public library. An experienced reference librarian knows that a few moments spent with the patron, listening, asking
questions, and listening some more, can go a long way in efficiently direct-
ing the user to the source that will fulfill the user's information needs. In
the computerized world of searchable databases this same strategy is being
developed, but it has a long way to go before being perfected.

There is another problem with locating the relevant documents for a respective query, and that is the increasing size of collections. Heretofore, the
focus of new technology has been more on processing and digitizing information, whether it be text, images, video, or audio, than on organizing it.

It has created a situation information designer Richard Saul Wurman [87] refers to as a *tsunami of data*:

> "This is a tidal wave of unrelated, growing data formed in bits and bytes, coming in an unorganized, uncontrolled, incoherent cacophony of foam. It's filled with flotsam and jetsam. It's filled with the sticks and bones and shells of inanimate and animate life. None of it is easily related, none of it comes with any organizational methodology."

To combat this tsunami of data, search engine designers have developed a set of mathematically based tools that will improve search engine performance. Such tools are invaluable for improving the way in which terms and documents are automatically synthesized. Term-weighting methods, for example, are used to place different emphases on a term's (or keyword's) relationship to the other terms and other documents in the collection. One of the most effective mathematical tools embraced in automated indexing is the vector space model [73].

In the vector space information retrieval (IR) model, a unique vector is defined for every term in every document. Another unique vector is computed for the user's query. With the queries being easily represented in the vector space model, searching translates to the computation of distances between query and document vectors. However, before vectors can be created in the document, some preliminary document preparation must be done.

1.1   Document File Preparation

Librarians are well aware of the necessities of organizing and extracting information. Through decades (or centuries) of experience, librarians have refined a system of organizing materials that come into the library. Every item is catalogued, based on some individual's or group's assessment of what that book is about, followed by appropriate entries in the library's on-line or card catalog. Although it is often outsourced, essentially each book in the library has been individually indexed or reviewed to determine its contents. This approach is generally referred to as *manual indexing*.

1.1.1   Manual Indexing

As with most approaches, there are are some real advantages and disadvantages to manual indexing. One major advantage is that a human indexer can establish relationships and concepts between seemingly different topics that can be very useful to future readers. Unfortunately, this task is expensive, time consuming, and can be at the mercy of the background and personality of the indexer. For example, studies by Cleverdon [24] reported that if two groups of people construct thesauri in a particular subject area, the overlap of index terms was only 60%. Furthermore, if two indexers used the same thesaurus on the same document, common index terms were shared in only 30% of the cases.

Also of potential concern is that the manually indexed system may not be reproducible or if the original system was destroyed or modified it would be difficult to recreate. All in all, it is a system that has worked very well, but with the continued proliferation of digitized information on the World Wide Web (WWW), there is a need for a more *automated* system.

Fortunately, because of increased computer processing power in this decade, computers have been used to extract and index words from documents in a more automated fashion. This has also changed the role of manual subject indexing. According to Kowalski [45], "The primary use of manual subject indexing now shifts to the abstraction of concepts and judgments on the value of the information."

Of course, the next stage in the evolution of automatic indexing is being able to link related concepts even when the query does not specifically make such a request.

1.1.2   File Cleanup

One of the least glamorous and often overlooked parts of search engine design is the preparation of the documents that are going to be searched. A simple analogy might be the personal filing system you may have in place at home. Everything from receipts to birth certificates to baby pictures are thrown into a filing cabinet or a series of boxes. It is all there, but without file folders, plastic tabs, color coding, or alphabetizing, it is nothing more than a heap of paper. Subsequently, when you go to search for the credit card bill you thought you paid last month, it is an exercise similar to rummaging through a wastebasket.

There is little difference between the previously described home filing system and documents in a web-based collection, especially if nothing has been done to standardize those documents to make them searchable. In other words, unless documents are cleaned up or purified by performing pedestrian tasks such as making sure every document has a title, marking where each document begins and ends, and handling parts of the documents that are not text (such as images), then most search engines will respond by returning the wrong document(s) or fragments of documents.

One misconception is that information that has been formatted through an hypertext markup language (HTML) editor and displayed in a browser is sufficiently formatted, but that is not always the case because HTML was designed as a platform-independent language. In general, web browsers are very forgiving with built-in error recovery and thus will display almost any kind of text, whether it looks good or not. However, search engines have more stringent format requirements, and that is why when building a web-based document collection for a search engine, each HTML document has to be validated into a more specific format prior to any indexing.

1.2   Information Extraction

In Chapter 2, we will go into more detail on how to go about doing this cleanup, which is just the first of many procedures needed for what is referred to as *item normalization*. We also look at how the words of a document are processed into searchable tokens by addressing such areas as processing tokens and stemming. Once these prerequisites are met, the documents are ready to be indexed.

1.3   Vector Space Modeling

SMART (system for the mechanical analysis and retrieval of text), developed by Gerald Salton and his colleagues at Cornell University [73], was one of the first examples of a vector space IR model. In such a model, both terms and/or documents are encoded as vectors in k-dimensional space. The choice k can be based on the number of unique terms, concepts, or perhaps classes associated with the text collection. Hence, each vector component (or dimension) is used to reflect the importance of the corresponding term/concept/class in representing the semantics or meaning of a document.

Figure 1.1 demonstrates how a simple vector space model can be represented as a *term-by-document* matrix. Here, each column defines a document, while each row corresponds to a unique term or keyword in the collection. The values stored in each matrix element or cell defines the frequency that a term occurs in a document. For example, *Term* 1 appears once in

	Document 1	Document 2	Document 3	Document 4
Term 1	1	0	1	0
Term 2	0	0	1	1
Term 3	0	1	1	0

Figure 1.1: Small term-by-document matrix.

both *Document* 1 and *Document* 3 but not in the other two documents (see Figure 1.1). Figure 1.2 demonstrates how each column of the 3×4 matrix in Figure 1.1 can be represented as a vector in 3-dimensional space. Using a k-dimensional space to represent documents for clustering and query matching purposes can become problematic if k is chosen to be the number of terms (rows of matrix in Figure 1.1). Chapter 3 will discuss methods for representing term-document associations in lower-dimensional vector spaces and how to construct term-by-documents using term-weighting methods [27, 71, 79] to show the importance a term can have within a document or across the entire collection.

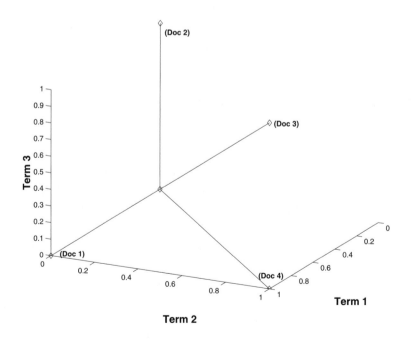

Figure 1.2: Representation of documents in a 3-dimensional vector space.

Through the representation of queries as vectors in the k-dimensional space, documents (and terms) can be compared and ranked according to similarity with the query. Measures such as the Euclidean distance and cosine of the angle made between document and query vectors provide the similarity values for ranking. Approaches based on conditional probabilities (logistic regression, Bayesian models) to judge document-to-query similarities are not the scope of *USE*; however, references to other sources such as [31, 32] have been included.

1.4   Matrix Decompositions

In simplest terms, search engines take the user's query and find all the documents that are related to the query. However, this task becomes complicated quickly, especially when the user wants more than just a literal match. One approach known as *latent semantic indexing* (LSI) [8, 25] attempts to do more than just literal matching. Employing a vector space representation of both terms and documents, LSI can be used to find relevant documents which may not even share any search terms provided by the user. Modeling the underlying term-to-document association patterns or relationships is the key for *conceptual*-based indexing approaches such as LSI.

The first step in modeling the relationships between the query and a document collection is just to keep track of which document contains which terms or which terms are found in which documents. This is a major task requiring computer-generated data structures (such as term-by-document matrices) to keep track of these relationships. Imagine a spreadsheet with every document of a database arranged in columns. Down the side of the chart is a list of all the possible terms (or words) that could be found in those documents. Inside the chart, rows of integers (or perhaps just ones and zeros) mark how many times the term appears in the document (or if it appears at all).

One interesting characteristic of term-by-document matrices is that they usually contain a greater proportion of zeros; i.e., they are quite *sparse*. Since every document will contain only a small subset of words from the dictionary, this phenomenon is not too difficult to explain. On the average, only about 1% of all the possible elements or cells are populated [8, 10, 43]. When a user enters a query, the retrieval system (search engine) will attempt to extract all matching documents. Recent advances in hardware technologies have produced extremely fast computers, but these machines are not so fast that they can scan through an entire database every time the user makes a query. Fortunately, through the use of concepts from applied mathematics, statistics, and computer science, the actual amount of information that must be processed to retrieve useful information is continuing to decrease. But such reductions are not always easy to achieve, especially if one wants to obtain more than just a literal match.

Efficiency in indexing via vector space modeling requires special encodings for terms and documents in a text collection. The encoding of term-by-document matrices for lower-dimensional vector spaces (where the dimension of the space is much smaller than the number of terms or documents) using either continuous or discrete matrix decompositions is required for LSI-based indexing. The singular value decomposition (SVD) [33] and semidiscrete decomposition (SDD) [43] are just two examples of the various matrix decompositions arising from numerical linear algebra that can be used in vector space IR models such as LSI. The matrix factors produced by these decompositions provide automatic ways of encoding or representing terms and documents as vectors in any dimension. The clustering of similar or related terms and documents is realized through probes into the derived vector space model, i.e., queries. A more detailed discussion of the use of matrix decompositions such as the SVD and SDD for IR models will be provided in Chapter 4.

1.5 Query Representations

Query matching within a vector space IR model can be very different from conventional item matching. Whereas the latter conjures up a image of a user typing in a few terms and the search engine matching the user's terms to those indexed from the documents in the collection, in vector space models such as LSI, the query can be interpreted as another (or new) document. Upon submitting the query, the search engine will retrieve the cluster of documents (and terms whose word usage patterns reflect that of the query).

This difference is not necessarily transparent to the experienced searcher. Those trained in searching are often taught Boolean searching methods (especially in library and information sciences), i.e., the connection of search terms by *AND* and *OR*. For example, if a Boolean searcher queries a CD-ROM encyclopedia on *German shepherds and bloodhounds*, the documents retrieved must have information about both German shepherds and blood-hounds. In a pure Boolean search, if the query was *German shepherds or bloodhounds*, the documents retrieved will include any article that has some-thing about German shepherds or bloodhounds.

IR models can differ in how individual search terms are processed. Typ-ically, all terms are treated equally with insignificant words removed. How-ever, some terms may be *weighted* according to their importance. Oddly enough, with vector space models, the user may be better off listing as many relevant terms as he or she can in the query, in contrast to a Boolean user who usually types in just a few words. In vector space models, the more terms that are listed, the better chance the search engine has in finding similar documents in the database.

Natural language queries such as "I would like articles about German Shepherds and bloodhounds" comprise yet another form of query represen-tation. Even though to the trained Boolean searcher this seems unnatural, this type of query can be easier and more accurate to process, because the importance of each word can be gauged from the semantic structure of the sentence. By discarding insignificant words (such as *I, would, like*) a conceptual-based IR system is able to determine which words are more important and therefore should be used to extract clusters of related docu-ments and/or terms.

In Chapter 5, we will further discuss the process of query binding, or how the search engine takes abstract formulations of queries and forms specific requests.

1.6   Ranking and Relevance Feedback

As odd as it may sound, search engine users really do not care how a search engine works; they are just interested in getting the information they have requested. Once they have the answer they want, they log off — end of query. This disregarding attitude creates certain challenges for the search engine builder. For example, only the user can ultimately judge if the retrieved information meets his or her needs. In information retrieval, this is known as *relevance*, or judging how well the information received matches the query. (Augmenting this problem is that oftentimes the user is not sure what he or she is looking for.) Fortunately, vector space modeling, because of its applied mathematical underpinnings, has characteristics which improve the chances that the user will eventually receive relevant documents to his or her corresponding query. The search engine does this in two ways: by ranking the retrieved documents according to how well they match the query and relevance feedback or asking the user to identify which documents best meet his or her information needs and then, based on that answer, resubmitting the query.

Applied mathematics plays such an integral part of vector-based search engines, because there is already in place a quantifiable way to say, *Document A ranks higher in meeting your criteria than Document B.* This idea can then be taken one step further, when the user is asked, *Do you want more documents like Document A or Document B or Document C...?* After the user makes the selection, more similar documents are retrieved and ranked. Again, this process is known as relevance feedback.

Using a more mathematical perspective, we will discuss in Chapter 6 the use of vector-based similarity measures (e.g., cosines) to rank-order documents (and terms) according to their similarity with a query.

1.7 Searching by Link Structure

As mentioned in the Preface, there are several different IR methods that can be used to build search engines. Although *USE* focuses on the mathematics of LSI, this method is limited to smaller document collections, and it is not readily scalable to handle a document collection the size of the Web. Methods that take into the account the hyperlink structure of the Web have already proven effective (and profitable). However, link structure-based algorithms are also dependent on linear algebra and graph theory. Chapter 7 looks at some of the math involved.

1.8 User Interface

If users are not particular about how search engines actually work, what really does matter to them? Is it just the search results? Not necessarily, as even the best possible search engine imaginable, guaranteed to produce great amounts of relevant documents for every query, would be underutilized if the user interface was extremely confusing. Conversely, how often have we returned to some ineffectual search engine time and time again just because it is easy to use? Probably more times than we are willing to admit.

These two extreme examples illustrate the importance of the user interface in search engine design. Usually on the Web, the user simply fills out a short form and then submits his or her query. But does the user know whether he or she is permitted to type in more than a few words, use Boolean operators, or if the query should be in the form of a question?

Other factors related to the user interface is how the retrieved documents will be displayed. Will it be titles only, titles and abstracts, or clusters of like documents? Then there is the issue of speed. Should the user ever be expected to wait more than five seconds for results after pressing the search key? In the design of search engines, there are trade-offs which will affect the speed of the retrieval. Chapter 8 includes features to consider when planning a search engine interface.

1.9 Book Format

Before we begin going into depth about each of the interrelated ingredients that goes into building a search engine, we want to remind the reader why the book is formatted the way it is. We are anticipating the likelihood that interested readers will have different backgrounds and viewpoints about search engines. Therefore, we purposely tried to separate the nontechnical material from the mathematical calculations. Those with an information sciences or nonmathematical background should consider skimming or skipping Chapters 3 and 4 and Sections 7.1 and 7.2. However, we encourage those with applied mathematics or computer science backgrounds to read the less technical Chapters 1, 2, 5, and 8 because the exposure to the information science perspective of search engines is critical for both assessing performance and understanding how users *see* search engines. In Chapter 9, we list background sources (including current websites) that not only have been influential in writing this book but can provide opportunities for further understanding.

Another point worth reminding readers about is that vector space modeling was chosen for conceptual IR to demonstrate the important role that applied mathematics can play in communicating new ideas and attracting multidisciplinary research in the design of intelligent search engines. Certainly there are other IR approaches, but hopefully our experiences with the vector space model will help pave the way for future system designers to build better, more useful search engines.

Chapter 2

Document File Preparation

As mentioned briefly in the introduction, a major part of search engine development is making decisions about how to prepare the documents that are to be searched. If the documents are automatically indexed, they will be managed much differently than if they were just manually indexed. The search engine designer must be aware that building the automatic index is as important as any other component of search engine development.

As pointed out by Korfhage in [44], system designers must also take into consideration that it is not unusual for a user to be linked into many different databases through a single user interface. Each one of these databases will often have its own way of handling the data. Also, the user is unaware that he or she is searching different databases (nor does he or she care). It is up to the search engine builder to smooth over these differences and make them transparent to the user.

Building an index requires two lengthy steps:

1. Document analysis and, for lack of a better word, *purification*. This requires analyzing how each document in each database (e.g., web documents) is organized in terms of what makes up a document (title, author or source, body) and how the information is presented. Is the critical information in the text, or is it presented in tables, charts, graphics, or images? Decisions must be made on what information or

11

parts of the document (referred to as *zoning* [45]) will be indexed and which information will not.

2. Token analysis or term extraction. On a word-by-word basis, a decision must be made on which words (or phrases) should be used as referents in order to best represent the semantic content (meaning) of documents.

2.1 Document Purification and Analysis

After even limited exposure to the Web, one quickly realizes that HTML documents are comprised of many attributes such as graphic images, photos, tables, charts, and audio clips — and those are just the visible characteristics. By viewing the source code of an HTML document, one also sees a variety of tags such as <TITLE>, <COMMENT>, and <META>, which are used to describe how the document is organized and displayed. Obviously, hypertext documents are *more* than just text.

Any search engine on the Web must address the heterogeneity of HTML documents. One of the changes in search engine development in the past few years is that instead of search engine developers adapting to the different types of webpages, webpage developers are adapting their webpages in order to woo the major commercial search engines. (See the sidebar on commercial search engines later in this chapter.) Since the publication of the first edition of *USE*, an entire cottage industry has emerged to specialize in what is known as search engine optimization (SEO), developing strategies to improve a site's position on the "results" page and translating that prominent position into more visits (clicks). Marketplace aside, search engines still must address the nonuniformity of processing HTML documents and make decisions on how to handle such nontextual elements as the following:

- <COMMENT> tags, which allow the page developer to leave hidden instructions or reminders about the page.

- <ALT TEXT>, an attribute which allows the page developer to provide a text description of an image in case the user has the browser set to *text only.*

- Uniform resource locators (URLs), which are usually defined within <HREF> tags.

- <FRAME>, an attribute that controls the layout and appearance of co-ordinated webpages.

- <META> tags, which are not part of the content but instead are used to describe the content. <META> description tags and <META> keywords both provide the developer an opportunity to be more specific on what each webpage is about.

In the past, some large web search engines deliberately avoided indexing some of the nontextual elements such as <META> tags to avoid problems/biases associated with the ranked returned list of documents. This was done to combat the web developers who would overload their <META> tags with keywords in hopes of skewing search results in their favor. This led to major search engines changing what they indexed and what they did not. And it is not unusual for these trends to change from time to time. For example, the major commerical search engines previously ignored <FRAME> and <ALT TEXT> during their crawling tasks, but this is no longer the case. Also, conventional wisdom (from a developer's standpoint, at least) still recommends that web authors pay attention to assigning values to the <META> keyword and description fields [69, 80].

2.1.1 Text Formatting

Before moving from step 1 of analyzing a document to step 2 of processing its individual elements, it is critical that each document be in ASCII or some similar (editable) format. This seems like a standard requirement, but one must remember that some documents are added into collections by optical character reader (OCR) scanners and may be recast in formats such as postscript. Such a format restricts searching because it exists more as an *image* rather than a collection of individual, searchable elements. Documents can be converted from postscript to ASCII files, even to the point that special and critical elements of the document such as the title, author, and date can be flagged and processed appropriately [44].

Search engine developers must also determine how they are going to index the text. Later, in the next section, we will discuss the process of item normalization (use of stop lists, stemmers, and the like), which is typically performed after the search engine has selected which text to index.

2.1.2   Validation

Producing *valid* HTML files, unfortunately, is not as straightforward as one
would expect. The lack of consistent tagging (by users) and nonstandard
software for HTML generation produces erroneous webpages that can make
both parsing and displaying a nightmare. On-line validation services, however, are making a difference in that users can submit their webpage(s) for
review and perhaps improve their skills in HTML development. An excellent resource for webpage/HTML validation is provided by the W3C HTML
Validation Service at `http://validator.w3.org/`. Users can submit the
URL of their webpage for validation.

To identify (or specify) which version of HTML is used within a particular webpage, the formal public identifier (FPI) comment line is commonly
used. A sample FPI declaration for the W3C 4.0 HTML syntax is provided
in Figure 2.1.

```
<!-- The first non-comment line is the FPI declaration for -->
<!-- this document. It declares to a parser and a human -->
<!-- reader the HTML syntax used in its creation. In this -->
<!-- example, the Document Type Definition (DTD) from the -->
<!-- W3C for HTML 4.0 was used during creation. It also -->
<!-- dictates to a parser what set of syntax rules to use -->
<!-- when validating. -->
<!DOCTYPE HTML PUBLIC "-//W3C//DTD HTML 4.0//EN">
<!DOCTYPE HTML PUBLIC "-//W3C//DTD HTML 4.0 Transitional//EN">
<HTML>
<HEAD>
<TITLE>Example</TITLE>
</HEAD>
<BODY>
...
</BODY>
</HTML>
```

Figure 2.1: FPI for HTML conforming to the W3C 4.0 standard.

2.2   Manual Indexing

Manual indexing, or indexing that is done by a person, connotes visions of
dedicated men and women willingly locked into small windowless rooms, sit-

ting at sparse desks hunched over stacks of papers, reading, and underlining keywords for the index. On coffee breaks, the indexers gather in the small break room and debate the nuances of language and exchange anecdotes about the surprising relationships between seemingly incongruent subjects.

Because of the exponential growth of the Web, from 320 million indexable pages in 1998 [53] to over four billion pages in 2004,[1] you would think that manual indexers must have gone the way of bank tellers and full service gas station attendants. In 2002, Yahoo! discontinued its practice of using manual indexers to look at submitted URLs before sending their crawlers out to index them. However, smaller web directories still exist on the Web, but they are characterized by their focus on specific topics rather than trying to index millions of pages. One upside of these smaller web subject directories is not only that the results are more relevant but also that human intervention greatly reduces "the probability of retrieving results out of context"[82].

In addition to the small web directories that still populate the Web, there are still major players in the information industry who prefer having documents analyzed individually. Some examples include the following:

- *National Library of Medicine.* The National Library of Medicine is the publisher of MEDLINE (Medical Literature, Analysis and Retrieval System Online), a bibliographic database of over 15 million references. Available free-of-charge on the Web via PubMed (www.pubmed.gov), MEDLINE relies heavily on freelance contractors located throughout the world to index half a million references annually. Only 27 of MEDLINE's 144 indexers are in-house staffers. Indexers assign keywords that match MeSH, the Medical Subject Headings Index. However, according to MEDLINE's Head of Indexing, James Marcetich, MEDLINE has added an automated indexer called the medical text indexer (MTI), which automatically indexes the title and abstract and gives the manual indexer some assistance by providing a list of potential MeSH keywords. (But not all of them use it, says Marcetich.) With an expected increase in workload (a million documents a year to index by 2011), Marcetich expects the MTI to play a more important role in the years to come.

---

[1]Estimating the size of the Web is anyone's educated guess. At the time of this writing, Google claimed over four billion pages indexed. Other estimates suggest that the "hidden" or "deep" Web, the maze of pages that are not readily available for crawling, could be easily over 500 billion pages [68].

- *H.W. Wilson Company.* H.W. Wilson Company, publishers of the *Readers' Guide to Periodical Literature* and other indexes, places major importance on having people assign subject headings. Working entirely out of the home office in Bronx, New York, 85 full-time indexers and editors add over 500,000 records to H.W. Wilson index publications annually. According to the Director of Indexing, Mark Gauthier, the publisher's indexing program is not machine-assisted but instead still relies on the "intellectual process of indexers." When the H.W. Wilson reevaluated their whole system from a cost perspective a couple years ago, it decided to concentrate its automation efforts on streamlining the process of getting information from the indexer to the publication rather than trying to replace manual indexing with automated indexing. "Our indexers are very fast, consistent and have a remarkable institutional memory," says Gauthier.

- *Cinahl.* The California-based Cinahl Information Systems manually indexes 1750 journals in the nursing and allied health disciplines, which includes such disciplines as physical and occupational therapy, alternative therapy, chiropractic medicine, gerontology, and biomedicine. The equivalent of 15 full-time indexers add 2500 to 3000 records a week to Cinahl's million-document database. Cinahl's Managing Director, June Levy, says that they have looked at automatic indexing software and will continue do so but only to assist their indexers and not replace them. Levy says that manual indexers are able to "pick up on the nuances of human language" that machines simply cannot do.

For the information industry to still make such an effort and expense to manually assign terms indicates the importance information professionals place in being able to recognize relationships and concepts in documents. It is this ability to identify the broader, narrower, and related subjects that keeps manual indexing a viable alternative in an industry that is somewhat dominated by automatic indexing. It also provides a goal for the automatic indexing system of being able to accurately forge relationships between documents that on the surface are not lexically linked.

2.3   Automatic Indexing

Automatic indexing, or using algorithms/software to extract terms for indexing, is the predominant method for processing documents from large web databases. In contrast to the connotation of manual indexers being holed up in their windowless rooms, the vision of automatic indexes consists of huge automatic computerized robots crawling throughout the Web all day and night, collecting documents and indexing every word in the text. This latter vision is probably as overly romanticized as the one for the manual indexers, especially considering that the robots are stationary and make requests to the servers in a fashion similar to a user making a request to a server.

Another difference between manual and automatic indexing is that concepts are realized in the indexing stage, as opposed to the document extraction/collection stage. This characteristic of automatic indexing places additional pressure on the search engine builder to provide some means of searching for broader, narrower, or related subjects. Ultimately, though, the goal of each system is the same: to extract from the documents the words which will allow a searcher to find the best documents to meet his or her information needs.

Major Commercial Search Engines

By looking at the features of some of major search engines such as Google, Yahoo!, and Ask Jeeves one can get a general idea of how major search engines do their automatic indexing. It can also offer insights on the types of decisions a search engine builder must make when extracting index terms.

Each search engine usually has its own *crawler*, which is constantly indexing millions of pages a day from the Web. While some crawlers just randomly search, others are specifically looking at previously indexed pages for updated information or are guided by user submissions. More heavily traveled websites are usually checked more often, whereas less popular websites may be visited only once a month.

While studying automatic indexing, keep in mind that the search engine or crawler *grabs* only part of the webpage and copies it into a more localized database. This means that when a user submits a query to the search engine, only that particular search engine's representation (or subset) of the Web is actually searched. Only then are you directed to the appropriate (current) URL. This explains in part why links from search results are invalid or redirected and the importance of search engines to update and refresh their existing databases.

Major Commercial Search Engines, contd.

However, there are limits to what search engines are willing or able to index per webpage. For example, Google's web crawler grabs around 100K of webpage text, whereas Yahoo! pulls about 500K [75]. Once webpages are *pulled in*, guidelines are set in advance on what exactly is indexed. Since most of the documents are written in HTML, each search engine must decide what to do with frames, password protected sites, comments, meta tags, and images. Search engine designers must determine which parts of the document are the best indicators of what the document is about for future ranking. Depending on the "philosophy" of the search engine, words from the <TITLE> and <META> tags are usually scrutinized as well as the links that appear on the page. Keeping counts or word frequencies within the entire document/webpage is essential for weighting the overall importance of words (see Section 3.2.1).

There are many reasons why search engines automatically index. The biggest reason is time. Besides, there is no way that the search engine could copy each of the millions of documents on the Web without exhausting available storage capacity. Another critical reason for using this method is to control how new documents are added to the collection. If one tried to "index on the fly" it would be difficult to control the flow of how new documents are added to the Web. Retrieving documents and building an index provides a manageable infrastructure for information retrieval and storage.

One of the most dramatic changes for major commercial search engines in the past several years has been the shift from using term weighting to link structure-based analysis to determine how pages rank when search results are returned. In other words, the more relevant pages are the ones that have authoritative pages that point to them. Moreover, these same relevant pages point to other authoritative pages. Google has taken these link structure-based techniques to become the major player in the commercial search engine marketplace [68].

By simply observing how current major search engines go about their business, search engine builders can glean two important bits of advice. One is to recognize the need of systematically building an index and how to control additions to the text corpus. Second, examining other search engines underscores the necessity of proper file preparation and cleanup.

2.4 Item Normalization

Building an index is more than just extracting words and building a data structure (e.g., term-by-document matrix) based on their occurrences. The words must be sliced and diced before being placed into any inverted file structure (see Section 2.5). This pureeing process is referred to as *item normalization*. Kowalski in [45] summarizes it as follows:

> "The first step in any integrated system is to normalize the incoming items to a standard format. In addition to translated multiple external formats that might be received into a single consistent data structure that can be manipulated by the functional processes, item normalization provides logical restructuring of the item. Additional operations during item normalization are needed to create a searchable data structure: identification of processing tokens (e.g., words), characterizations of tokens, and stemming (e.g., removing word endings) of the tokens. The original item or any of its logical subdivisions is available for the user to display. The processing tokens and their characterizations are used to define the searchable text from the total received text."

In other words, part of the document preparation is taking the smallest unit of the document, in most cases words, and constructing searchable data structures. Words are redefined as the symbols (letters, numbers) between interword symbols such as blanks. A searching system must make decisions on how to handle words, numbers, and punctuation. Documents are not just made up of words: they are composed of *processing tokens*. Identifying processing tokens constitutes the first part of item normalization. The characterization of tokens or *disambiguation* of terms (i.e., deriving the meaning of a word based on context) can be handled after normalization is complete.

A good illustration of the effort and resources required to characterize tokens automatically can be found in the National Library of Medicine's unified medical language system (UMLS) project. For over a decade, the UMLS has been working on enabling computer systems to *understand* medical meaning [64]. The *Metathesaurus* is one of the components of the UMLS and contains half a million biomedical concepts with over a million different concept names. Obviously, to do this, automated processing of the machine-readable versions of its 40 source vocabularies is necessary, but it also requires review and editing by subject experts.

The next step in item normalization is applying stop lists to the collection of processing tokens. Stop lists are lists of words that have little or no value as a search term. A good example of a stop list is the list of stop words from the SMART system at Cornell University (see `ftp://ftp.cs.cornell.edu/pub/smart/english.stop`). Just a quick scroll through this list of words (able, about, after, allow, became, been, before, certainly, clearly, enough, everywhere, etc.) reveals their limited impact in discriminating concepts or potential search topics. From the data compression viewpoint, stop lists eliminate the need to handle unnecessary words and reduce the size of the index and the amount of time and space required to build searchable data structures.

However, the value of removing stop words for a compressed inverted file is questionable [86]. Applying a stop list does reduce the size of the index, but the words that are omitted are typically those that require the fewest bits per pointer to store so that the overall savings in storage is not that impressive.

Although there is little debate over eliminating common words, there is some discussion on what to do about *singletons* or words that appear only once or very infrequently in a document or a collection. Some indexers may feel that the probability of searching with such a term is small or the importance of a such a word is so minimal that it should be included in the stop list also.

Stemming, or the removing of suffixes (and sometimes prefixes) to reduce a word to its root form, has a relatively long tradition in the index building process. For example, words from a document database such as *reformation, reformative, reformatory, reformed, and reformism* can all be stemmed to the root word *reform* (perhaps a little dangerous to remove the *re-* prefix). All five words would map to the word *reform* in the index. This saves the space of four words in the index. However, if a user queries for information about the *Reformation* and some of the returned documents describe *reformatories* (i.e., reform schools), it could leave the user scratching his or her head wondering about the quality of the search engine. If the query from the user is stemmed, there are advantages and disadvantages also. Stemming would help the user if the query was misspelled and stemming handles the plurals and common suffixes, but again there is always the risk that stemming will cause more nonrelevant items to be pulled more readily from the database. Also stemming proper nouns, such as the words that originate from database fields like *author*, is usually not done.

Stemming can be done in various ways, but it is not a task to be regarded lightly. Stemming can be a tedious undertaking, especially considering that decisions must be made and rules developed for thousands of words in the English language. Fortunately, several automatic stemmers utilizing different approaches have been developed. As suggested by [44, 45, 86], the Porter Stemmer is one of the industry stalwarts. A public domain version (written in C) is available for downloading at `http://www.tartarus.org/~martin/PorterStemmer/index.html`. The Porter Stemmer approach is based on the sequences of vowels and consonants, whereas other approaches follow the general principle of *looking up* the stem in a dictionary and assigning the stem that best represents the word.

2.5 Inverted File Structures

One of the universal linchpins of all information retrieval and database systems is the inverted file structure (IFS), a series of three components that track which documents contain which index terms. IFSs provide a critical shortcut in the search process. Instead of searching the entire document database for specific terms in a query, the IFS organizes the information into an abbreviated list of terms, which then, depending on the term, references a specific set of documents. It is just like picking up a geography reference book and looking for facts about the *Appalachian Mountains*. You can turn page by page and eventually find your facts, or you can check the index, which immediately directs you to the pages that have facts about the *Appalachian Mountains*. Both methods work, but the latter is usually much quicker.

As mentioned earlier, there are three components in the IFS:

- The *document file* is where each document is given a unique number identifier and all the terms (processing tokens) within the document are identified.

- The *dictionary* is a sorted list of all the unique terms (processing tokens) in the collection along with pointers to the *inversion list*.

- The *inversion list* contains the pointer from the term to which documents contain that term. (In a book index, the *pointer* would be the page number where the term *Appalachian* would be found.)

To illustrate the use of the IFS, we have created a two-stanza limerick about a searcher and her query.

Bread Search
There once was a searcher named Hanna,
Who needed some info on manna.
She put "rye" and "wheat" in her query
Along with "potato" or "cranbeery,"
But no mention of "sourdough" or "banana."

Instead of rye, cranberry, or wheat,
The results had more spiritual meat.
So Hanna was not pleased,
Nor was her hunger eased,
'Cause she was looking for something to eat.

2.5.1   Document File

The first step in creating the IFS is extracting the terms that should be used in the index and assigning each document a unique number. For simplicity's sake each line of the limerick can be used to represent a document (see Table 2.1). Not only is the punctuation removed, but keep in mind that common, often-used words have little value in searching and thus reside in the stop lists and are not pulled for the index. This means that a significant

Table 2.1: Documents (records) defined by limerick.

1	There once was a searcher named Hanna
2	Who needed some info on manna
3	She put rye and wheat in her query
4	Along with potato or cranbeery
5	But no mention of sourdough or banana
6	Instead of rye cranberry or wheat
7	The results had more spiritual meat
8	So Hanna was not pleased
9	Nor was her hunger eased
10	Cause she was looking for something to eat

percentage of the words are not indexed, reducing the storage space requirements for the system. Even so, for purposes of this example, we were liberal in selecting terms to be used in the index (see Table 2.2).

Table 2.2: Terms extracted (parsed) from limerick.

Doc. No.	Terms/Keywords
1	searcher, Hanna
2	manna
3	rye, wheat, query
4	potato, cranbeery[a]
5	sourdough, banana
6	rye, cranberry[a], wheat
7	spiritual, meat
8	Hanna
9	hunger
10	*No terms*

[a]The words *cranberry* and *cranbeery* would probably stem to the same root word, *cranb*. This illustrates the value of stemming if a word is misspelled or the writer of the document — in this case the poet — has taken *too much license*.

2.5.2 Dictionary List

The second step would be to extract the terms and create a searchable dictionary of terms. To facilitate searching, the terms could be arranged alphabetically; however, there are other time and storage saving strategies that can be implemented. Instead of whole words, the processing tokens are broken down to a letter-by-letter *molecular level* for specific data structure implementations, that is, a reorganization of the data in such a way to allow more efficient searching. Two well-known data structures for processing dictionaries are N-grams and PAT trees. Kowalski [45] gives an overview of both methods and includes references for more understanding, but for the purposes of explaining IFSs, it is unnecessary to go into more detail.

Sometimes the dictionary list might also indicate the number of times the term appears in the document database, such as the list for the *Bread Search* document collection created in Table 2.3.

Table 2.3: Dictionary list for the limerick.

Term	Global Frequency
banana	1
cranb	2
Hanna	2
hunger	1
manna	1
meat	1
potato	1
query	1
rye	2
sourdough	1
spiritual	1
wheat	2

2.5.3   Inversion List

The final step in building an IFS is to combine the dictionary list and the document list to form what is called the *inversion list*. The inversion list *points* to a specific document(s) when a term is selected. For the limerick example, if the query contained the term *wheat*, documents (lines) 3 and 6 will be retrieved. In addition to pointing to a specific document, inverted lists can be constructed to *point* to a particular *zone* or section of the document where the term is used. Table 2.4 illustrates how both the document and position of a term can be recorded in the inverted list. Notice that the first occurrence of the word *wheat* is in document 3 at position 5 (i.e., it is the fifth word).

Inverted lists can certainly be more sophisticated than what has been described thus far, especially when the search engine must support contiguous word phrases. A *contiguous word phrase* is used when specific word combinations are requested by the user. Using the frustrated searcher Hanna, let us say she queried on *banana bread*. In other words, she wants to pull only documents where the word *banana* is next to the word *bread*. If the inverted list stores the position of each word, then such a determination can be made. Some systems are designed to measure how close terms are to each other, i.e., their *proximity*. For example, a user might want documents that contain only *banana* if it is within five words of *bread*. Obviously, it is a

Table 2.4: Inversion list for the limerick example.

Term	(Doc. No., Position)
banana	(5,7)
cranb	(4,5); (6,4)
Hanna	(1,7); (8,2)
hunger	(9,4)
manna	(2,6)
meat	(7,6)
potato	(4,3)
query	(3,8)
rye	(3,3); (6,3)
sourdough	(5,5)
spiritual	(7,5)
wheat	(3,5); (6,6)

useful feature, and many systems can do this, but there is a slight trade-off in systems that support contiguous word phrases and proximity measures — higher storage requirements and computational costs.

Also there is no hard and fast rule that only one inverted file system can be created for a document collection. Separate IFSs can be developed for different zones or portions of the documents such as the title or abstract. An inverted file system could be built just for authors with a special set of rules such as no stop lists. This allows the user to search quicker on specific fields within the database.

Besides serving as an example of an IFS and reinforcing the adage that life does imitate art — or in this case life imitates bad poetry — *Bread Search* also illustrates the blur between searching for concepts and more concrete items. In *Bread Search*, Hanna could have been searching a biblical database about manna, the bread-like food provided by God to the Israelites during their exodus from Egypt. But *manna* has conceptual connotations as well, mainly as a metaphor of something that can be spiritually nourishing. Perhaps in a future search in the same biblical database, Hanna could be looking for activities that give a person spiritual nourishment and regeneration — the bread of life. Hopefully, Hanna's results will include more than just recipes.

2.5.4   Other File Structures

While the IFS is commonly used to build an index, there are other approaches. One alternative is the use of *signature files* in which words/terms are converted into binary strings (composed of zeros and ones). Words from a query are mapped to their signatures, and the search involves matching bit positions with the (precomputed) signatures of the items/documents. In one sense, the *signature file* takes an opposite approach compared to the IFS. Whereas the IFS matches the query with the term, the signature file eliminates all nonmatches. After superimposing different signature files, the query signature is compared, and the nonmatches fall by the wayside. In general, the documents corresponding to the remaining signatures are then searched to see if the query terms do indeed exist in those documents.

Figure 2.2 illustrates how one of the verses (ignoring punctuation) from the limerick in Section 2.5 might be encoded as a *block* signature. Here, the first three characters of each word/term in the verse are translated into 8-bit strings according to the hash function $f(c) = 2^{(c \bmod 8)}$, where the value c is the octal value of the corresponding ASCII character. The four-word signatures are OR'ed to create the block signature for the verse (document). To avoid signatures which are overly dense with 1's, a maximum number of

Term	Octal Values per Character (c)		
Nor	116	157	162
her	150	145	162
hun*ger*	150	165	156
eas*ed*	145	141	163

Term	$f(c) = 2^{(c \bmod 8)}$		
Nor	01 000 000	10 000 000	00 000 100
her	00 000 001	00 100 000	00 000 100
hun*ger*	00 000 001	00 100 000	00 100 000
eas*ed*	00 100 000	00 000 010	00 001 000
Block Signature	01 100 001	10 100 010	00 101 100

Figure 2.2: Block signature construction.

words per block is typically specified, and documents are partitioned into blocks of that size [45]. Also, a maximum number (m) of 1's that may be specified per word is defined ($m = 3$ in Figure 2.2). Query terms are mapped to their respective signatures, and then bit positions in all signatures (query and documents) are compared to delineate nonmatches. A technique referred to as *Huffman coding* is a well-documented approach for encoding symbols/words, given a certain probability distribution for the symbols [86].

Although the binary strings can become fairly large, blocking can be used to combine signatures and thus facilitate searching. One variation of the signature file is the *bitmap*. For a particular document, every bit associated with a term used in that document is set to one. All other bits are set to zero. For lengthy documents, very long binary strings will be produced, and the exhaustive storage requirements for large document collections can render this approach impractical.

According to [86] signature files require more space than compressed inverted files and are typically designed to handle large conventional databases. A more in-depth discussion of the intricacies and specific usefulness of signature files can be found in [29].

Chapter 3

Vector Space Models

As first mentioned in Section 1.3, a vector space model can be used to encode/represent both terms and documents in a text collection. In such a model, each component of a document vector can be used to represent a particular term/keyword, phrase, or concept used in that document. Normally, the value assigned to a component reflects the importance of the term, phrase, or concept in representing the *semantics* of the document (see Section 3.2.1).

3.1 Construction

A document collection comprised of n documents which are indexed by m terms can be represented as an $m \times n$ *term-by-document matrix* A. The n (column) vectors representing the n documents form the columns of the matrix. Thus, the matrix element a_{ij} is the weighted frequency at which term i occurs in document j [8]. Using the vector space model, the columns of A are interpreted as the *document vectors*, and the rows of A are considered the *term vectors*.

The column space of A essentially determines the semantic content of the collection; i.e., the document vectors span the content. However, it is not the case that every vector represented in the column space of A has a specific interpretation. For example, a linear combination of any two document vectors does not necessarily represent a viable document from the collection. More importantly, the vector space model can exploit geometric relationships between document (and term) vectors in order to explain both similarities and differences in concepts.

3.1.1 Term-by-Document Matrices

For heterogeneous text collections, i.e., those representing many different contexts (or topics) such as newspapers and encyclopedias, the number of terms (m) is typically much greater than the number of documents ($n \ll m$). For the Web, however, the situation is reversed. Specifically, a term-by-document matrix using the words of the largest English language dictionary as terms and the set of all webpages as documents would be about $300,000 \times 4,000,000,000$ [4, 13, 53, 68]. Since any one document will consist of only a small subset of words from the entire dictionary (associated with the particular database), the majority of elements defining the term-by-document matrix will be zero.

Figure 3.1 demonstrates how a 9×7 term-by-document matrix is constructed from a small collection of book titles.[2] In this simple example, only a subset (underlined) of all the words used in the 7 titles were chosen terms/keywords for indexing purposes. The stop list (see Section 2.4) in this case would contain words like *First*, *Aid*, *Room*, etc. Notice that any particular term occurs only once in any given document. Certainly for larger collections, the term frequencies can be considerably larger than 1 for any document. As the semantic content of a document is generally determined by the *relative* frequencies of terms, the elements of the term-by-document matrix A are sometimes scaled so that the Euclidean norm (or vector 2-norm) of each column is 1. Recall that the Euclidean vector norm $\|x\|_2$ is defined by

$$\|x\|_2 = \sqrt{x^T x} = \sqrt{\sum_{i=1}^{m} x_i^2},$$

where $x = (x_1, x_2, \ldots, x_m)$. For example, with each column a_j of the matrix A in Figure 3.1 we have $\|a_j\|_2 = 1$, $j = 1, \ldots, 7$. As will be discussed in Section 3.2.1, the actual values assigned to the elements of the term-by-document matrix $A = [a_{ij}]$ are usually *weighted* frequencies, as opposed

---

[2]These *actual* book titles were obtained using the search option at `www.amazon.com`.

	Terms		*Documents*
T1:	Bab(y,ies,y's)	D1:	Infant & Toddler First Aid
T2:	Child(ren's)	D2:	Babies & Children's Room
			(For Your Home)
T3:	Guide	D3:	Child Safety at Home
T4:	Health	D4:	Your Baby's Health and Safety:
T5:	Home		From Infant to Toddler
T6:	Infant	D5:	Baby Proofing Basics
T7:	Proofing	D6:	Your Guide to Easy Rust Proofing
T8:	Safety	D7:	Beanie Babies Collector's Guide
T9:	Toddler		

The 9×7 term-by-document matrix before normalization, where the element $\hat{a}_{ij}$ is the number of times term i appears in document title j:

$$\hat{A} = \begin{pmatrix} 0 & 1 & 0 & 1 & 1 & 0 & 1 \\ 0 & 1 & 1 & 0 & 0 & 0 & 0 \\ 0 & 0 & 0 & 0 & 0 & 1 & 1 \\ 0 & 0 & 0 & 1 & 0 & 0 & 0 \\ 0 & 1 & 1 & 0 & 0 & 0 & 0 \\ 1 & 0 & 0 & 1 & 0 & 0 & 0 \\ 0 & 0 & 0 & 0 & 1 & 1 & 0 \\ 0 & 0 & 1 & 1 & 0 & 0 & 0 \\ 1 & 0 & 0 & 1 & 0 & 0 & 0 \end{pmatrix}$$

The 9×7 term-by-document matrix with unit columns:

$$A = \begin{pmatrix} 0 & 0.5774 & 0 & 0.4472 & 0.7071 & 0 & 0.7071 \\ 0 & 0.5774 & 0.5774 & 0 & 0 & 0 & 0 \\ 0 & 0 & 0 & 0 & 0 & 0.7071 & 0.7071 \\ 0 & 0 & 0 & 0.4472 & 0 & 0 & 0 \\ 0 & 0.5774 & 0.5774 & 0 & 0 & 0 & 0 \\ 0.7071 & 0 & 0 & 0.4472 & 0 & 0 & 0 \\ 0 & 0 & 0 & 0 & 0.7071 & 0.7071 & 0 \\ 0 & 0 & 0.5774 & 0.4472 & 0 & 0 & 0 \\ 0.7071 & 0 & 0 & 0.4472 & 0 & 0 & 0 \end{pmatrix}$$

Figure 3.1: The construction of a term-by-document matrix A.

to the *raw* counts of term occurrences (within a document or across the entire collection).

As illustrated in Figure 3.1, not all the words are used to describe the collection of book titles. Only those words related to *child safety* were selected. Determining which words to index and which words to discard defines both the *art* and the *science* of automated indexing. Using lexical matching, no title would be retrieved for a user searching for titles on *First Aid*. Both the words *First* and *Aid* would have to be added to the index (i.e., create two new rows for the term-by-document matrix) in order to retrieve book title D1.

In constructing a term-by-document matrix, terms are usually identified by their word stems (see Section 2.4). In the example shown in Figure 3.1, the words *Baby*, *Babies*, and *Baby's* are counted as 1 term, and the words *Child* and *Children* are treated the same. Stemming, in these situations, reduces the number of rows in the term-by-document matrix A from 12 to 9. The reduction of storage (via stemming) is certainly an important consideration for large collections of documents.

Even with this tiny sample of book titles, we find evidence of two of the most common (and major) obstacles to the retrieval of relevant information: *synonymy* and *polysemy*. Synonymy refers to the use of synonyms, or different words that have the same meaning, and polysemy refers to words that have different meanings when used in varying contexts. Four of the nine terms indexed in Figure 3.1 are synonyms: *Baby*, *Child*, *Infant*, and *Toddler*. Examples of *polysemous* words include *Proofing* (child or rust) and *Babies* (human or stuffed). Methods for handling the effects of synonymy and polysemy in the context of vector space models are considered in Section 3.2.

3.1.2   Simple Query Matching

The small collection of book titles from Figure 3.1 can be used to illustrate simple query matching in a low-dimensional space. Since there are exactly 9 terms used to index the 7 book titles, queries can be represented as 9×1 vectors in the same way that each of the 7 titles is represented as a column of the 9×7 term-by-document matrix A. In order to retrieve books on *Child Proofing* from this small collection, the corresponding query vector would be

$$q = \begin{pmatrix} 0 & 1 & 0 & 0 & 0 & 0 & 1 & 0 & 0 \end{pmatrix}^T;$$

that is, the frequencies of the terms *Child* and *Proofing* in the query would specify the values of the appropriate nonzero entries in the query vector.

Query matching in the vector space model can be viewed as a search in the column space of the matrix A (i.e., the subspace *spanned* by the document vectors) for the documents most similar to the query. One of the most common similarity measures used for query matching in this context is the *cosine* of the angle between the query vector and the document vectors. If we define a_j as the jth document vector (or the jth column of the term-by-document matrix A), then the cosines between the query vector $q = (q_1, q_2, \ldots, q_m)^T$ and the $n = 7$ document vectors are defined by

$$\cos \theta_j = \frac{a_j^T q}{\|a_j\|_2 \|q\|_2} = \frac{\displaystyle\sum_{i=1}^{m} a_{ij} q_i}{\sqrt{\displaystyle\sum_{i=1}^{m} a_{ij}^2} \sqrt{\displaystyle\sum_{i=1}^{m} q_i^2}} \tag{3.1}$$

for $j = 1, \ldots, n$. Since the query vector and document vectors are typically *sparse* (i.e., have relatively few nonzero elements), computing the inner products and norms in equation (3.1) is not that expensive. Also, notice that the document vector norms $\|a_j\|_2$ can be precomputed and stored before any cosine computation. If the query and document vectors are normalized (see Section 3.2.1) so that $\|q\|_2 = \|a_j\|_2 = 1$, the cosine calculation constitutes a single inner product. More information on alternative similarity measures is provided in [38, 83].

In practice [8], documents whose corresponding document vectors produce cosines (with the query vector) greater than some threshold value (e.g., $|\cos \theta_j| \geq 0.5$) are judged as relevant to the user's query. For the collection of book titles in Figure 3.1, the nonzero cosines are $\cos \theta_2 = \cos \theta_3 = 0.4082$ and $\cos \theta_5 = \cos \theta_6 = 0.5000$. Hence, a cosine threshold of 0.5 would judge only the fifth and sixth documents as relevant to *Child Proofing*. While the fifth document is certainly relevant to the query, clearly the sixth document (concerning *rust* proofing) is irrelevant. While the seventh document is correctly ignored, the first four documents would not be returned as relevant.

If one was interested in finding books on *Child Home Safety* from the small collection in Figure 3.1, the only nonzero cosines made with the query vector

$$\tilde{q} = \begin{pmatrix} 0 & 1 & 0 & 0 & 1 & 0 & 0 & 1 & 0 \end{pmatrix}^T$$

would be $\cos\theta_2 = 0.6667$, $\cos\theta_3 = 1.0000$, and $\cos\theta_4 = 0.2582$. With a cosine threshold of 0.5, the first, fourth, and fifth documents (which are relevant to the query) would not be returned.

Certainly, this representation of documents solely based on term frequencies does not adequately model the semantic content of the book titles. Techniques to improve the vector space representation of documents have been developed to address the *errors* or uncertainty associated with this *basic* vector space IR model. One approach is based on the use of term weights (see Section 3.2.1), and another approach relies on computing low-rank approximations to the original term-by-document matrix. The premise of the latter approach is based on the potential *noise* reduction (due to problems like synonymy and polysemy) achieved by low-rank approximation. Vector space IR models such as LSI [7, 8, 25] rely on such approximations to encode both terms and documents for conceptual-based query matching. Following [7], the process of *rank reduction* can be easily explained using numerical algorithms such as the QR factorization and SVD [33], which are typically presented in linear algebra textbooks. We will discuss these important numerical methods in the context of IR modeling in Chapter 4.

3.2   Design Issues

3.2.1   Term Weighting

A collection of n documents indexed by m terms (or keywords) can be represented as an $m \times n$ term-by-document matrix $A = [a_{ij}]$ (see Section 3.1.1). Each element, a_{ij}, of the matrix A is usually defined to be a *weighted* frequency at which term i occurs in document j [8, 71]. The main purpose for term weighting is to improve retrieval performance. Performance in this case refers to the ability to retrieve relevant information (recall) and to dismiss irrelevant information (precision). As will be discussed in Section 6.1, *recall* is measured as the ratio of the number of relevant documents retrieved to the total number of relevant items which exist in the collection, and *precision* is measured as the ratio of the number of relevant documents retrieved to the total number of documents retrieved. A desirable IR system is one which achieves high precision for most levels of recall (if not all). One way to improve recall for a given query is to use words with high frequency, i.e., those which appear in many documents in the collection. In contrast, obtaining high precision may require the use of very specific terms or words that will match the most relevant documents in the collection. No doubt some sort of compromise must be made to achieve sufficient recall without poor precision. Term weighting is one approach commonly used to improve the retrieval performance of automatic indexing systems.

Using a format similar to that presented in [43], let each element a_{ij} be defined by

$$a_{ij} = l_{ij} g_i d_j, \qquad (3.2)$$

where l_{ij} is the local weight for term i occurring in document j, g_i is the global weight for term i in the collection, and d_j is a document normalization factor which specifies whether or not the columns of A (i.e., the documents) are normalized. Tables 3.1 through 3.3 contain some of the popular weight formulas used in automated indexing systems. For convenience [43], let

$$\chi(r) = \begin{cases} 1 & \text{if } r > 0, \\ 0 & \text{if } r = 0, \end{cases}$$

define f_{ij} as the number of times (frequency) that term i appears in document j, and let $p_{ij} = f_{ij} / \sum_j f_{ij}$.

Table 3.1: Formulas for local term weights (l_{ij}).

Symbol	Name	Formula
b	Binary [71]	$\chi(f_{ij})$
l	Logarithmic [34]	$\log(1 + f_{ij})$
n	Augmented normalized term frequency [34, 71]	$(\chi(f_{ij}) + (f_{ij}/\max_k f_{kj}))/2$
t	Term frequency [71]	f_{ij}

A simple notation for specifying a term-weighting scheme is to use the three-letter string associated with the particular local, global, and normalization factors desired. For example, the *lfc* weighting scheme defines

$$a_{ij} = \frac{\log(f_{ij} + 1) \; \log\left(n / \sum_j \chi(f_{ij})\right)}{\sqrt{\sum_i \left(\log(f_{ij} + 1) \; \log\left(n / \sum_j \chi(f_{ij})\right)\right)^2}}.$$

Table 3.2: Formulas for global term weights (g_i).

Symbol	Name	Formula
x	None	1
e	Entropy [27]	$1 + \left(\sum_j (p_{ij} \log(p_{ij})) / \log n \right)$
f	Inverse document frequency (IDF) [27, 71]	$\log \left(n / \sum_j \chi(f_{ij}) \right)$
g	GfIdf [27]	$\left(\sum_j f_{ij} \right) / \sum_j \chi(f_{ij})$
n	Normal [27]	$1 / \sqrt{\sum_j f_{ij}^2}$
p	Probabilistic inverse [34, 71]	$\log \left(\left(n - \sum_j \chi(f_{ij}) \right) / \sum_j \chi(f_{ij}) \right)$

Table 3.3: Formulas for document normalization (d_j).

Symbol	Name	Formula
x	None	1
c	Cosine [71]	$\left(\sum_i (g_i l_{ij})^2 \right)^{-1/2}$

Defining an appropriate weighting scheme from the choices in Tables 3.1 through 3.3 certainly depends on certain characteristics of the document collection [71]. The choice for the local weight (l_{ij}) may well depend on the vocabulary or word usage patterns for the collection. For technical or scientific vocabularies (e.g., technical reports and journal articles), schemes of the form *nxx* with normalized term frequencies are generally recommended. For more general (or varied) vocabularies (e.g., popular magazines and encyclopedias), simple term frequencies (*t**) may be sufficient. Binary term frequencies (*b**) are useful when the term list (or row dimension of the term-by-document matrix) is relatively short, such as the case with *controlled vocabularies*.

Choosing the global weighting factor (g_i) should take into account the state of the document collection. By this we mean how often the collection is likely to change. Adjusting the global weights in response to new vocabulary will impact all the corresponding rows of the term-by-document matrix. To avoid updating, one may simply disregard the global factor (*x**) altogether. For more static collections, the IDF global weight (*f**) is a common choice among automatic indexing systems [27, 71].

It has been observed that the probability that a document being judged relevant by a user significantly increases with document length [78]. In other words, the longer a document is, the more likely all the keywords will be found (and with higher frequency). As demonstrated for SMART [22], experiments with document length normalization have demonstrated that the traditional cosine normalization (**c*) is not particularly effective for large full text documents (e.g, TREC-4). In order to retrieve documents of a certain length with the same probability of retrieving a relevant document of that same length, the recent *Lnu* or *pivoted-cosine* normalization scheme [22, 78] has been proposed for indexing the TREC collections. This scheme is based on the assignment

$$a_{ij} = \frac{(1 + \log(f_{ij}))/(1 + \log(\bar{f}_{ij}))}{(1 - s) \times p + s \times u},$$

where $\bar{f}_{ij} = (\sum_i f_{ij})/(\sum_i \chi(f_{ij}))$, s is referred to as the *slope* and is typically set to 0.2, p is the *pivot* value, which is defined to be the average number of *unique* terms/keywords occurring (per document) throughout the collection, and u is the number of unique terms in document j. In effect, this formula is an adjustment to cosine normalization so that relevant documents of smaller size will have a better chance of being judged similar. In TREC-3 experiments [78], the *Lnu* weighting scheme employing *pivoted-cosine* normalization obtained 13.7% more relevant documents (for 50 queries) compared with a comparable weighting scheme based on the more traditional cosine normalization. What this result indicates is that document relevance

and length should not be considered mutually independent with respect to
retrieval performance.

3.2.2   Sparse Matrix Storage

As discussed in Sections 1.3 and 3.1.1, the number of nonzeros defined within
term-by-document matrices is relatively small compared with the number of
zeros. Such sparse matrices generally lack any particular nonzero structure
or pattern, such as *banded* 10×6 matrix A illustrated by

$$A = \begin{pmatrix} x & x & & & & \\ x & x & & & & \\ & x & x & & & \\ & & x & x & & \\ & & x & x & & \\ & & & x & x & \\ & & & x & x & \\ & & & x & x & \\ & & & & x & x \\ & & & & x & x \end{pmatrix}.$$

If a term-by-document matrix had a (banded) nonzero element structure
similar to that above, the ability to identify *clusters* of documents sharing
similar terms would be quite simplified. Obtaining such matrices for general
text is quite difficult; however, some progress in the reordering of hypertext-
based matrices has been made [9].

In order to avoid both the storage and processing of zero elements, a variety of sparse matrix storage formats have been developed [3]. In order to
allocate contiguous storage locations in memory for the nonzero elements,
a sparse matrix format must *know* exactly how the elements *fit* into the
complete (or full) term-by-document matrix. Two formats that are suitable
for term-by-document matrices are compressed row storage (CRS) and compressed column storage (CCS). These sparse matrix formats do not make
any assumptions on the nonzero structure (or pattern) of the matrix. CRS
places the nonzeros of the matrix rows into contiguous storage (arrays),
and the CCS format stores the matrix columns in similar fashion. To im-
plement either format requires three arrays of storage that can be used to
access/store any nonzero. The contents of these arrays for both the CRS
and CCS formats are described below.

Compressed Row Storage

This sparse matrix format requires one floating-point array (`val`) for storing the nonzero values (i.e., weighted or unweighted term frequencies) and two additional integer arrays for indices (`col_ind`, `row_ptr`). The `val` array stores the nonzero elements of the term-by-document matrix A as they are traversed row-wise, i.e., stores all the frequencies (in order from left to right) of the current term before moving on to the next one. The `col_ind` array stores the corresponding column indices (document numbers) of the elements (term frequencies) in the `val` array. Hence, `val`$(k) = a_{ij}$ implies `col_ind`$(k) = j$. The `row_ptr` array stores the locations of the `val` array (term frequencies) that begin a row. If `val`$(k) = a_{ij}$, then `row_ptr`(i) $\leq k \leq$ `row_ptr`$(i+1)$. If nnz is the number of nonzero elements (term frequencies) for the term-by-document matrix A, then it is customary to define `row_ptr`$(n+1) = nnz + 1$. It is easy to show that the difference `row_ptr`$(i+1)$ − `row_ptr`(i) indicates how many nonzeros are in the ith row of the matrix A, i.e., the number of documents associated with the ith term/keyword. For an $m \times n$ term-by-document matrix, the CRS format requires only $2nnz + m + 1$ storage (array) locations compared with mn for the complete (includes zeros) matrix A.

Compressed Column Storage

The CCS format is almost identical to the CRS format in that the columns of the matrix A (as opposed to the rows) are stored in contiguous (array) locations. The CCS format, which is the CRS format for the transpose of the matrix A (i.e., A^T), is also known as the *Harwell–Boeing* sparse matrix format (see [26]). The three arrays required for the CCS format are {`val`, `row_ind`, `col_ptr`}, where `val` stores the the nonzero elements of the term-by-document matrix A as they are traversed columnwise, i.e., stores all the frequencies (in order from top to bottom) of the each document. The `row_ind` array stores the corresponding row indices (term numbers or identifiers) of the elements (term frequencies) in the `val` array. Hence, `val`(k) $= a_{ij}$ implies `row_ind`$(k) = i$. The `col_ptr` array with CCS stores the locations of the `val` array (term frequencies) that begin a column (document) so that `val`$(k) = a_{ij}$ indicates that `col_ptr`$(j) \leq k \leq$ `col_ptr`$(j+1)$. Figure 3.2 illustrates the three arrays needed for the CRS and CCS representations of the 9×7 term-by-document matrix A in Figure 3.1.

CRS			CCS		
val	col_ind	row_ptr	val	row_ind	col_ptr
0.5774	2	1	0.7071	6	1
0.4472	4	5	0.7071	9	3
0.7071	5	7	0.5774	1	6
0.7071	7	9	0.5774	2	9
0.5774	2	10	0.5774	5	14
0.5774	3	12	0.5774	2	16
0.7071	6	14	0.5774	5	18
0.7071	7	16	0.5774	8	20
0.4472	4	18	0.4472	1	
0.5774	2	20	0.4472	4	
0.5774	3		0.4472	6	
0.7071	1		0.4472	8	
0.4472	4		0.4472	9	
0.7071	5		0.7071	1	
0.7071	6		0.7071	7	
0.5774	3		0.7071	3	
0.4472	4		0.7071	7	
0.7071	1		0.7071	1	
0.4472	4		0.7071	3	

Figure 3.2: CRS and CCS representations of the 9×7 term-by-document matrix A ($nnz = 19$) from Figure 3.1.

3.2.3   Low-Rank Approximations

The process of indexing (whether manual or automated) may well be considered an art rather than a science. The uncertainties associated with term-by-document matrices can largely be attributed to differences in language (word choice) and culture. Errors in measurement can accumulate and thereby generate *uncertainty* in the experimental data. Fundamental differences in word usage between authors and readers suggest that there will never be a *perfect* term-by-document matrix that accurately represents all possible term-document associations. As an example, notice that document D4: Your Baby's Health and Safety: From Infant to Toddler from the small collection of book titles in Figure 3.1 would be a good match for a search on books for *Child Proofing*. This judgment of *relevance* would suggest that the unnormalized matrix $\hat{A}$ in Figure 3.1 should have the entries $\hat{a}_{24} = \hat{a}_{74} = 1$. Since the true association of terms (and concepts) to documents is subject to many interpretations, the term-by-document matrix A may be better represented [7] by the matrix sum $A + E$, where E reflects the *error* or *uncertainty* in assigning (or generating) the elements of matrix A.

It can be shown that the 9×7 term-by-document matrix for the small collection of book titles in Figure 3.1 has rank 7. In other words, the matrix has exactly 7 linearly independent columns (or document vectors in this case) [33]. For larger text collections and especially the Web, the corresponding $m \times n$ matrix A may not have *full* rank (i.e, n linearly independent columns). In fact, if the book title

     D8: <u>Safety</u> <u>Guide</u> for <u>Child</u> <u>Proofing</u> Your <u>Home</u>

was added to the collection in Figure 3.1, the unnormalized matrix $\hat{A}$ would still have rank 7. In other words, both the matrix $\hat{A}$ given by

$$\hat{A} = \begin{pmatrix} 0 & 1 & 0 & 1 & 1 & 0 & 1 & 0 \\ 0 & 1 & 1 & 0 & 0 & 0 & 0 & 1 \\ 0 & 0 & 0 & 0 & 0 & 1 & 1 & 1 \\ 0 & 0 & 0 & 1 & 0 & 0 & 0 & 0 \\ 0 & 1 & 1 & 0 & 0 & 0 & 0 & 1 \\ 1 & 0 & 0 & 1 & 0 & 0 & 0 & 0 \\ 0 & 0 & 0 & 0 & 1 & 1 & 0 & 1 \\ 0 & 0 & 1 & 1 & 0 & 0 & 0 & 1 \\ 1 & 0 & 0 & 1 & 0 & 0 & 0 & 0 \end{pmatrix}$$

and the normalized term-by-document matrix A defined as

$$A = \begin{pmatrix} 0 & 0.5774 & 0 & 0.4472 & 0.7071 & 0 & 0.7071 & 0 \\ 0 & 0.5774 & 0.5774 & 0 & 0 & 0 & 0 & 0.4472 \\ 0 & 0 & 0 & 0 & 0 & 0.7071 & 0.7071 & 0.4472 \\ 0 & 0 & 0 & 0.4472 & 0 & 0 & 0 & 0 \\ 0 & 0.5774 & 0.5774 & 0 & 0 & 0 & 0 & 0.4472 \\ 0.7071 & 0 & 0 & 0.4472 & 0 & 0 & 0 & 0 \\ 0 & 0 & 0 & 0 & 0.7071 & 0.7071 & 0 & 0.4472 \\ 0 & 0 & 0.5774 & 0.4472 & 0 & 0 & 0 & 0.4472 \\ 0.7071 & 0 & 0 & 0.4472 & 0 & 0 & 0 & 0 \end{pmatrix}$$

would still have 7 linearly independent columns (document vectors).

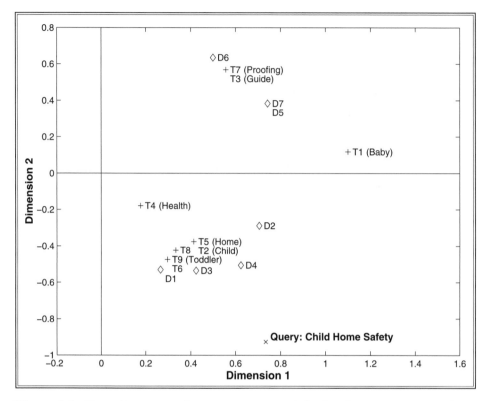

Figure 3.3: Two-dimensional representation of the book title collection from Figure 3.1.

Recent approaches to facilitate conceptual indexing, i.e., the ability to find relevant information without requiring literal word matches, have focused on the use of rank-k approximations to term-by-document matrices [7, 12, 43]. LSI [8, 25] is one popular approach which uses such approximations to encode m terms and n documents in k-dimensional space, where $k \ll \min(m, n)$. As illustrated in Figure 3.3, a rank-2 approximation to the matrix A from Figure 3.1 can be used to represent[3] both terms and documents in two dimensions. Unlike the traditional vector space model, the coordinates produced by low-rank approximations do not *explicitly* reflect term frequencies within documents. Instead, methods such as LSI attempt

---

[3]As the truncated SVD used to produce this rank-2 approximation is unique [33] up to the signs of the resulting term and document vector elements, an equivalent (mirrored) plot would have the query coordinates as $(-0.7343, 0.9269)$ rather than $(0.7343, -0.9269)$.

to model *global* usage patterns of terms so that related documents which may not share common (literal) terms are still represented by nearby vectors in a k-dimensional subspace. The grouping of terms (or documents) in the subspace serves as an automated approach for *clustering* information according to concepts [45]. From Figure 3.3, the separation of book titles in two dimensions reflects both the isolated use of terms such as *Guide* and *Proofing* and the used synonyms such as *Baby, Child, Infant,* and *Toddler.* Notice that the vector representation of the query *Child Home Safety* is clearly in the direction of the document cluster {D1, D2, D3, D4}. In fact, the largest cosine values between the query vector and all document vectors produced by the rank-2 approximation are $\cos\theta_3 = 1.000$, $\cos\theta_4 = 0.9760$, $\cos\theta_1 = 0.9788$, and $\cos\theta_2 = 0.8716$. In contrast to the simple query matching discussed in Section 3.1.2, this particular IR model would return the first and fourth documents as relevant to the query. The fifth document, however, would still be missed even with this improved encoding method. Determining the optimal rank to encode the original term-by-document matrix A is an open question [8] and is certainly database-dependent. In order to understand just how the coordinates shown in Figure 3.3 are produced, we turn our attention to matrix factorizations that can be used to produce these low-rank approximations.

Chapter 4

Matrix Decompositions

To produce a reduced-rank approximation of an $m \times n$ term-by-document matrix A, one must first be able to identify the dependence between the columns or rows of the matrix A. For a rank-k matrix A, the k basis vectors of its column space serve in place of its n column vectors to represent its column space.

4.1 QR Factorization

One set of basis vectors is found by computing the QR factorization of the term-by-document matrix

$$A = QR, \tag{4.1}$$

where Q is an $m \times m$ orthogonal matrix and R is an $m \times n$ upper triangular matrix. Recall that a square matrix Q is *orthogonal* if its columns are orthonormal. In other words, if q_j denotes a column of the orthogonal matrix Q, then q_j has unit Euclidean norm ($\|q_j\|_2 = \sqrt{q_j^T q_j} = 1$ for $j = 1, 2, \ldots, m$), and it is orthogonal to all other columns of Q ($\sqrt{q_j^T q_i} = 0$ for all $i \neq j$.) The rows of Q are also orthonormal, meaning that $Q^T Q = QQ^T = I$. The factorization of the matrix A in equation (4.1) exists for any matrix A, and [33] surveys the various methods for computing the QR factorization. Given the relation $A = QR$, it follows that the columns of the matrix A are all linear combinations of the columns of Q. Thus, a subset of k of the columns of Q form a *basis* for the column space of A, where $k = \text{rank}(A)$.

The QR factorization in equation (4.1) can be used to determine the basis vectors for any term-by-document matrix A. For the 9×7 term-by-document matrix in Figure 3.1, the factors are

$$
Q[:,1:5] = \begin{pmatrix}
0 & -0.5774 & 0.5164 & -0.4961 & 0.1432 \\
0 & -0.5774 & -0.2582 & 0.2481 & -0.0716 \\
0 & 0 & 0 & 0 & 0 \\
0 & 0 & 0 & -0.6202 & -0.2864 \\
0 & -0.5774 & -0.2582 & 0.2481 & -0.0716 \\
-0.7071 & 0 & 0 & 0 & 0 \\
0 & 0 & 0 & 0 & 0.9309 \\
0 & 0 & -0.7746 & -0.4961 & 0.1432 \\
-0.7071 & 0 & 0 & 0 & 0
\end{pmatrix},
$$

$$
Q[:,6:9] = \begin{pmatrix}
-0.1252 & 0.3430 & 0 & 0 \\
0.0626 & -0.1715 & -0.5962 & 0.3802 \\
0.9393 & 0.3430 & 0 & 0 \\
0.2505 & -0.6860 & 0 & 0 \\
0.0626 & -0.1715 & 0.5962 & -0.3802 \\
0 & 0 & -0.3802 & -0.5962 \\
0.1252 & -0.3430 & 0 & 0 \\
-0.1252 & 0.3430 & 0 & 0 \\
0 & 0 & 0.3802 & 0.5962
\end{pmatrix}, \qquad (4.2)
$$

$$
R = \begin{pmatrix}
-1 & 0 & 0 & -0.6325 & 0 & 0 & 0 \\
0 & -1 & -0.6667 & -0.2582 & -0.4082 & 0 & -0.4082 \\
0 & 0 & -0.7454 & -0.1155 & 0.3651 & 0 & 0.3651 \\
0 & 0 & 0 & -0.7211 & -0.3508 & 0 & -0.3508 \\
0 & 0 & 0 & 0 & 0.7596 & 0.6583 & 0.1013 \\
0 & 0 & 0 & 0 & 0 & 0.7528 & 0.5756 \\
0 & 0 & 0 & 0 & 0 & 0 & 0.4851 \\
0 & 0 & 0 & 0 & 0 & 0 & 0 \\
0 & 0 & 0 & 0 & 0 & 0 & 0
\end{pmatrix}, \qquad (4.3)
$$

where $Q[:, i : j]$ refers to columns i through j of matrix Q using MATLAB [60] indexing notation.

Notice how the first 7 columns of Q are partitioned (or separated) from the others in equation (4.2). Similarly, the first 7 rows of the matrix R in equation (4.3) are partitioned from the bottom 2×7 zero submatrix. The QR factorization of this term-by-document matrix can then be represented as

$$A = (Q_1 \quad Q_2) \begin{pmatrix} R_1 \\ 0 \end{pmatrix}$$

$$= Q_1 R_1 + Q_2 \cdot 0 = Q_1 R_1, \tag{4.4}$$

where Q_1 is the 9×7 matrix defining the first 7 columns of Q, Q_2 is the 9×2 remaining submatrix of Q, and R_1 reflects the *nonzero* rows of R. This partitioning clearly reveals that the columns of Q_2 will not contribute any nonzero values to inner products associated with the multiplication of factors Q and R to produce the matrix A. Hence, the ranks (i.e., the number of independent columns) of the 3 matrices A, R, and R_1 are the same, so that the first 7 columns of Q constitute a basis for the column space of A.

As discussed in [7], the partitioning of the matrix R above into zero and nonzero submatrices is not always automatic. In many cases, *column pivoting* is needed during the QR factorization to guarantee the zero submatrix at the bottom of R (see [33] for more details).

One motivation for computing the QR factorization of the term-by-document matrix A is that the basis vectors (of the column space of A) can be used to describe the *semantic* content of the corresponding text collection. The cosines of the angles θ_j between a query vector q and the document vectors a_j (for $j = 1, 2, \ldots, n$) are given by

$$\cos \theta_j = \frac{a_j^T q}{\|a_j\|_2 \|q\|_2} = \frac{(Q_1 r_j)^T q}{\|Q_1 r_j\|_2 \|q\|_2} = \frac{r_j^T (Q_1^T q)}{\|r_j\|_2 \|q\|_2}, \tag{4.5}$$

where r_j refers to column j of the submatrix R_1. Since multiplication of a vector by a matrix having orthonormal columns does not alter the norm of the vector, we can write

$$\|Q_1 r_j\|_2 = \sqrt{(Q_1 r_j)^T Q_1 r_j} = \sqrt{r_j^T Q_1^T Q_1 r_j} = \sqrt{r_j^T I r_j} = \sqrt{r_j^T r_j} = \|r_j\|_2.$$

For the term-by-document matrix from Figure 3.1 and the query vector q (*Child Proofing*) we observe no loss of information in using the factorization in equation (4.1). Specifically, the nonzero cosines computed via equation (4.5) are identical with those computed using equation (3.1): $\cos \theta_2 = \cos \theta_3 = 0.408248$ and $\cos \theta_5 = \cos \theta_6 = 0.500000$.

Since the upper triangular matrix R and the original term-by-document matrix A have the same rank, we now focus on how the QR factorization can be used to produce a low-rank approximation (see Section 3.2.3) to A. Given any term-by-document matrix A, its rank is not immediately known. The rank of the corresponding matrix R from the QR factorization of A, however, is simply the number of nonzero elements on its diagonal. With column pivoting, a permutation matrix P is generated so that $AP = QR$ [7], and the large and small elements of the matrix R (in magnitude) are *separated*, i.e., moving the larger entries toward the upper left corner of the matrix and the smaller ones toward the lower right. If successful, this separation essentially partitions the matrix R so that the submatrix of smallest elements is completely isolated.

With column pivoting, the matrix R in equation (4.3) is replaced by

$$
R = \left(
\begin{array}{ccccc|cc}
-1 & 0 & 0 & -0.4082 & -0.4082 & -0.2582 & -0.6667 \\
0 & -1 & 0 & 0 & 0 & -0.6325 & 0 \\
0 & 0 & -1 & -0.5000 & -0.5000 & 0 & 0 \\
0 & 0 & 0 & -0.7638 & -0.1091 & -0.2760 & 0.3563 \\
0 & 0 & 0 & 0 & 0.7559 & 0.2390 & -0.3086 \\
\hline
0 & 0 & 0 & 0 & 0 & 0.6325 & 0.4082 \\
0 & 0 & 0 & 0 & 0 & 0 & -0.4082 \\
0 & 0 & 0 & 0 & 0 & 0 & 0 \\
0 & 0 & 0 & 0 & 0 & 0 & 0 \\
\end{array}
\right) \quad (4.6)
$$

$$
= \begin{pmatrix} R_{11} & R_{12} \\ 0 & R_{22} \end{pmatrix}.
$$

The submatrix R_{22} above is a relatively small part of the matrix R. In fact, $\|R_{22}\|_F / \|R\|_F = 0.8563/2.6458 = 0.3237$, where the Frobenius matrix norm ($\|\cdot\|_F$) of a real $m \times n$ matrix $B = [b_{ij}]$ is defined [33] by

$$
\|B\|_F = \sqrt{\sum_{i=1}^{m} \sum_{j=1}^{n} b_{ij}^2}.
$$

If we redefine the submatrix R_{22} to be the 4×2 zero matrix, then the modified upper triangular matrix $\tilde{R}$ has rank 5 rather than 7. The matrix $A + E = Q\tilde{R}$ also has rank 5, where $E = (A + E) - A$. The perturbation or *uncertainty* matrix E can be defined as

$$
\begin{aligned}
E &= (A + E) - A \\
&= Q \begin{pmatrix} R_{11} & R_{12} \\ 0 & 0 \end{pmatrix} - Q \begin{pmatrix} R_{11} & R_{12} \\ 0 & R_{22} \end{pmatrix} \\
&= Q \begin{pmatrix} 0 & 0 \\ 0 & -R_{22} \end{pmatrix},
\end{aligned}
$$

so that $\|E\|_F = \|R_{22}\|_F$. Since $\|E\|_F = \|R_{22}\|_F$, $\|E\|_F/\|A\|_F = \|R_{22}\|_F/\|R\|_F = 0.3237$. Hence, the relative change of about 32% in the matrix R yields the same change in the matrix A, and the rank of these two matrices is reduced from 7 to 5. As discussed in [7] and [35], studies have indicated that discrepancies in indexing (same document indexed by different professional indexers) can account for some of the uncertainty (around 20%) in IR modeling. To account for this uncertainty or *noise* in the original term-by-document matrix (A), lower-rank approximations ($A + E$) can be constructed (as shown above) so that small perturbations (E) are relatively small. Also, computing cosines via equation (4.5) requires the factorization $Q\tilde{R}$, as opposed to the (explicit) matrix $A + E$.

Returning to our small collection of book titles in Figure 3.1, suppose we replace the original term-by-document matrix A by the perturbed matrix $A + E$ defined above. Keep in mind that the rank of $A + E = Q\tilde{R}$ is now 5, as opposed to 7. The factors Q, $\tilde{R}$, and permutation matrix P produced by column pivoting on the original term-by-document matrix A are

$$
Q = \begin{pmatrix}
-0.5774 & 0 & 0 & -0.6172 & 0.5345 \\
-0.5774 & 0 & 0 & 0.3086 & -0.2673 \\
0 & 0 & -0.7071 & 0.4629 & 0.5345 \\
0 & 0 & 0 & 0 & 0 \\
-0.5774 & 0 & 0 & 0.3086 & -0.2673 \\
0 & -0.7071 & 0 & 0 & 0 \\
0 & 0 & -0.7071 & -0.4629 & -0.5345 \\
0 & 0 & 0 & 0 & 0 \\
0 & -0.7071 & 0 & 0 & 0
\end{pmatrix},
$$

$$\tilde{R} \;=\; \begin{pmatrix} -1 & 0 & 0 & -0.4082 & -0.4082 & -0.2582 & -0.6667 \\ 0 & -1 & 0 & 0 & 0 & -0.6325 & 0 \\ 0 & 0 & -1 & -0.5000 & -0.5000 & 0 & 0 \\ 0 & 0 & 0 & -0.7638 & -0.1091 & -0.2760 & 0.3563 \\ 0 & 0 & 0 & 0 & 0.7559 & 0.2390 & -0.3086 \end{pmatrix}, \; \text{and}$$

$$P \;=\; \begin{pmatrix} 0 & 1 & 0 & 0 & 0 & 0 & 0 \\ 1 & 0 & 0 & 0 & 0 & 0 & 0 \\ 0 & 0 & 0 & 0 & 0 & 0 & 1 \\ 0 & 0 & 0 & 0 & 0 & 1 & 0 \\ 0 & 0 & 0 & 1 & 0 & 0 & 0 \\ 0 & 0 & 1 & 0 & 0 & 0 & 0 \\ 0 & 0 & 0 & 0 & 1 & 0 & 0 \end{pmatrix}.$$

Using the above factors and equation (4.5), the cosines with respect to the query vector q (*Child Proofing*) are very similar to those reported in Section 3.1.2: $\cos\theta_2 = 0.408248$ and $\cos\theta_3 = \cos\theta_5 = \cos\theta_6 = 0.500000$. For the query vector $\tilde{q}$ (*Child Home Safety*), the rank-5 representation of $A + E$ produces only 2 nonzero cosines, $\cos\theta_2 = 0.666667$ and $\cos\theta_3 = 0.816497$, so that the previous similarity with document D4 (albeit rather small) has been lost. With a cosine threshold of 0.5 (see Section 3.1.2), we would pick up the relevant document D3 for the query q but lose the relevant document D4 for query $\tilde{q}$. Hence, minor rank reduction does not necessarily improve matching for all queries.

If we wanted to further reduce the rank of R in equation (4.7), we might include both the fifth row and column in R_{22}. In this situation, we would have $\|R_{22}\|_F / \|R\|_F = 0.7559$ so that the discarding of R_{22} for a rank-4 approximation of the original term-by-document matrix A would produce a relative change of almost 76%. The nonzero cosines for the query vector q mentioned above would be $\cos\theta_2 = 0.408248$, $\cos\theta_3 = 0.308607$, $\cos\theta_4 = 0.183942$, $\cos\theta_5 = \cos\theta_6 = 0.500000$, and $\cos\theta_7 = 0.654654$. Although the relevant document D4 is now barely similar to the query (*Child Proofing*), we find that the completely unrelated document D7 is now judged as the most similar.

For the query vector $\tilde{q}$ (*Child Home Safety*), the rank-4 approximation produces the nonzero cosines $\cos\theta_2 = 0.666667$, $\cos\theta_3 = 0.755929$, $\cos\theta_4 = 0.100125$, and $\cos\theta_7 = 0.356348$. Here again, an increase in the number of irrelevant documents (D7) matched may coincide with attempts to match documents (D4) previously missed with larger ranks. Explanations as to why one variant (rank reduction) of a term-by-document matrix works better than another for particular queries are not consistent. As further discussed in [7], it is possible to improve the performance of a vector space IR model (e.g., LSI) by reducing the rank of the term-by-document matrix A. Note that even the 32% change in A used above for the rank-5 approximation can be considered quite large in the context of scientific or engineering applications where accuracies of three or more decimal places (0.1% error or better) are needed.

4.2 Singular Value Decomposition

In Section 4.1, we demonstrated the use of the QR factorization to generate document vectors of any specific dimension. While this approach does provide a reduced-rank basis for the column space of the term-by-document matrix A, it does not provide any information about the row space of A. In this section, we introduce an alternate SVD-based approach (although more demanding from a computational standpoint), which provides reduced-rank approximations to both spaces. Furthermore, the SVD has the unique mathematical feature of providing the rank-k approximation to a matrix A of minimal change for any value of k.

The SVD of the $m \times n$ term-by-document matrix A is written

$$A = U\Sigma V^T,$$

where U is the $m \times m$ orthogonal matrix whose columns define the left singular vectors of A, V is the $n \times n$ orthogonal matrix whose columns define the right singular vectors of A, and Σ is the $m \times n$ diagonal matrix containing the singular values $\sigma_1 \geq \sigma_2 \geq \cdots \geq \sigma_{\min(m,n)}$ of A in order along its diagonal. We note that this factorization exists for any matrix A and that methods for computing the SVD of both dense [33] and sparse matrices (see Chapter 9) are well documented. The relative sizes of the factors U, Σ, and V for the cases $m > n$ and $m < n$ are illustrated in Figure 4.1. All off-diagonal elements of the Σ matrix are zeros.

Both the SVD $A = U\Sigma V^T$ and the QR factorization $AP = QR$ can be used to reveal the rank (r_A) of the matrix A. Recall that r_A is the

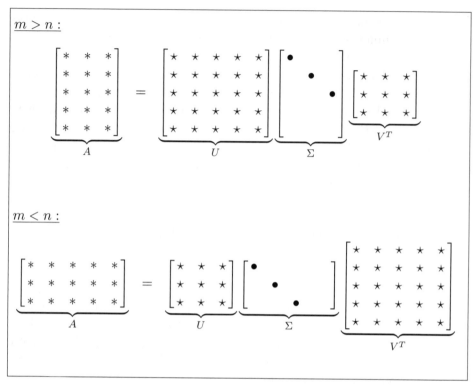

Figure 4.1: Component matrices of the SVD [7].

number of nonzero diagonal elements of R. Similarly, r_A is also the number of nonzero diagonal elements of Σ. Whereas the first r_A columns of Q form a basis for the column space,[4] so do the first r_A columns of U. Since a rank-k approximation to A, where $k \leq r_A$, can be constructed by ignoring (or setting equal to zero) all but the first k rows of R, we can define an alternative rank-k approximation (A_k) to the matrix A by setting all but the k-largest singular values of A equal to zero. As discussed in [7, 8], this approximation is in fact the *closest* rank-k approximation to A according to a theorem by Eckart and Young in [28, 62]. This theorem demonstrated that the error in approximating A by A_k is given by

$$\|A - A_k\|_F = \min_{\mathrm{rank}(B)\leq k} \|A - B\|_F = \sqrt{\sigma_{k+1}^2 + \cdots + \sigma_{r_A}^2}, \qquad (4.7)$$

---

[4]The first r_A rows of V^T form a basis for the row space of A.

where $A_k = U_k \Sigma_k V_k^T$, U_k and V_k comprise the first k columns of U and V, respectively, and Σ_k is the $k \times k$ diagonal matrix containing the k-largest singular values of A. In other words, the error in approximating the original term-by-document matrix A by A_k is determined by the truncated (or discarded) singular values $(\sigma_{k+1}, \sigma_{k+2}, \ldots, \sigma_{r_A})$.

The SVD of the matrix A in Figure 3.1 is $A = U \Sigma V^T$, where

$$
U[:, 1:5] = \begin{pmatrix}
0.6977 & 0.0931 & -0.0175 & 0.6951 & 0 \\
0.2619 & -0.2966 & -0.4681 & -0.1969 & 0 \\
0.3527 & 0.4491 & 0.1017 & -0.4013 & -0.7071 \\
0.1121 & -0.1410 & 0.1478 & 0.0733 & 0 \\
0.2619 & -0.2966 & -0.4681 & -0.1969 & 0 \\
0.1874 & -0.3747 & 0.5049 & -0.1270 & 0 \\
0.3527 & 0.4491 & 0.1017 & -0.4013 & 0.7071 \\
0.2104 & -0.3337 & -0.0954 & -0.2820 & 0 \\
0.1874 & -0.3747 & 0.5049 & -0.1270 & 0
\end{pmatrix},
$$

$$
U[:, 6:9] = \begin{pmatrix}
-0.0157 & -0.1441 & 0 & 0 \\
0.2468 & 0.1570 & -0.6356 & 0.3099 \\
0.0066 & 0.0493 & 0 & 0 \\
-0.4842 & 0.8402 & 0 & 0 \\
0.2468 & 0.1570 & 0.6356 & -0.3099 \\
0.2287 & -0.0338 & -0.3099 & -0.6356 \\
0.0066 & 0.0493 & 0 & 0 \\
-0.7340 & -0.4657 & 0 & 0 \\
0.2287 & -0.0338 & 0.3099 & 0.6356
\end{pmatrix},
$$

$$
\Sigma = \begin{pmatrix}
1.5777 & 0 & 0 & 0 & 0 & 0 & 0 \\
0 & 1.2664 & 0 & 0 & 0 & 0 & 0 \\
0 & 0 & 1.1890 & 0 & 0 & 0 & 0 \\
0 & 0 & 0 & 0.7962 & 0 & 0 & 0 \\
0 & 0 & 0 & 0 & 0.7071 & 0 & 0 \\
0 & 0 & 0 & 0 & 0 & 0.5664 & 0 \\
0 & 0 & 0 & 0 & 0 & 0 & 0.1968 \\
0 & 0 & 0 & 0 & 0 & 0 & 0 \\
0 & 0 & 0 & 0 & 0 & 0 & 0
\end{pmatrix},
$$

$$
V[:, 1:5] = \begin{pmatrix}
0.1680 & -0.4184 & 0.6005 & -0.2256 & 0 \\
0.4471 & -0.2280 & -0.4631 & 0.2185 & 0 \\
0.2687 & -0.4226 & -0.5009 & -0.4900 & 0 \\
0.3954 & -0.3994 & 0.3929 & 0.1305 & 0 \\
0.4708 & 0.3028 & 0.0501 & 0.2609 & 0.7071 \\
0.3162 & 0.5015 & 0.1210 & -0.7128 & 0 \\
0.4708 & 0.3028 & 0.0501 & 0.2609 & -0.7071
\end{pmatrix},
$$

$$
V[:, 6:7] = \begin{pmatrix}
0.5710 & -0.2432 \\
0.4872 & 0.4986 \\
-0.2451 & -0.4451 \\
-0.6132 & 0.3697 \\
-0.0113 & -0.3405 \\
0.0166 & 0.3542 \\
-0.0113 & -0.3405
\end{pmatrix}.
$$

This matrix A (of rank $r_A = 7$) has 7 nonzero singular values, and the 2 trailing zero rows of the diagonal matrix Σ indicate that the first 7 columns of U (i.e., U_1, U_2, ..., U_7) determine a basis for the column space of A. From equation (4.7), we know that $\|A - A_6\|_F = \sigma_4 = 0.1968$ so that $\|A - A_6\|_F / \|A\|_F \approx 0.0744$ for $\|A\|_F = 2.6458$. Hence, producing a rank-6 approximation to the original matrix A reflects only a 7% relative change from A. Reductions to rank 5 and rank 3 would reflect relative changes of 23% and 46%, respectively. If changes of 46% are deemed too large (compared to the initial uncertainty in the original term-by-document matrix A), then modest rank reductions (say from 7 to 5) may be more appropriate for this small text collection.

To accept a 5-dimensional subspace and the corresponding matrix A_5 as the *best* representation of the semantic structure of a collection/database implies that any further rank reduction will not model the *true* content of the collection. The choice of rank that produces the *optimal* performance of LSI (for any database) remains an open question and is normally decided via empirical testing [7, 8]. For very large databases, the number of dimensions used may be between 100 and 300 [57]. The choice here is typically governed by *computational feasibility*, as opposed to accuracy. Keep in mind that among all possible rank-k matrix approximations to A, the matrix A_k via SVD factors does produce the *best* approximation.

4.2.1 Low-Rank Approximations

Recall from Section 4.1 that relative changes of 32% and 76% were required to reduce the rank of the matrix A from Figure 3.1 to 5 and 4, respectively. Using the SVD, the relative changes required for reductions to ranks 5 and 4 are considerably less, i.e., 23% and 35%. As pointed out in [7], a visual comparison of the rank-reduced approximations to A can be misleading. Notice the similarity of the rank-4 QR-based approximation ($\tilde{A}_4$) to the original term-by-document matrix A in Figure 4.2. The more accurate SVD-based approximation (A_4) is only mildly similar to A.

It is interesting to note that (by construction) the term-by-document matrix A will have nonnegative elements (weighted frequencies) (see Section 3.1.1). From Figure 4.2, we see that both A_4 and $\tilde{A}_4$ have negative elements (which reflect various linear combinations of the elements of the matrix A). While this may seem problematic, the individual components of document vectors (columns of A_k) are not typically used to define semantic content. In other words, the *geometric* relationships between vectors (e.g., cosines) in the vector space are used to model concepts spanned by both terms and documents (see Section 3.2.3). Notice, for example, that the first document vector (column) in the rank-4 matrix A_4 has (positive) components associated with terms which did not occur in the original document D1: $A_4(4,1) = 0.1968$ and $A_4(8,1) = 0.2151$. The vector representation of this document (D1: Infant & Toddler First Aid) now has components associated with the relevant terms T4: Health and T8: Safety. This ability to automatically associate related terms (without human intervention) is the hallmark of vector space modeling and motivation for low-rank approximation techniques.

4.2.2 Query Matching

As was done for the QR factorization in Section 4.1, query matching can be formulated using the component matrices of the SVD. This particular formulation is the foundation of vector space IR models such as LSI (see Chapter 3). Suppose we want to compare the query vector q to the columns of the reduced-rank matrix A_k (as opposed to the original $m \times n$ term-by-document matrix A). Suppose the vector e_j denotes the jth canonical vector of dimension n (i.e., the jth column of the $n \times n$ identity matrix I_n). Then, it follows that the vector $A_k e_j$ is simply the jth column of the rank-k matrix A_k.

The original 9×7 term-by-document matrix A is

$$\begin{pmatrix}
0 & 0.5774 & 0 & 0.4472 & 0.7071 & 0 & 0.7071 \\
0 & 0.5774 & 0.5774 & 0 & 0 & 0 & 0 \\
0 & 0 & 0 & 0 & 0 & 0.7071 & 0.7071 \\
0 & 0 & 0 & 0.4472 & 0 & 0 & 0 \\
0 & 0.5774 & 0.5774 & 0 & 0 & 0 & 0 \\
0.7071 & 0 & 0 & 0.4472 & 0 & 0 & 0 \\
0 & 0 & 0 & 0 & 0.7071 & 0.7071 & 0 \\
0 & 0 & 0.5774 & 0.4472 & 0 & 0 & 0 \\
0.7071 & 0 & 0 & 0.4472 & 0 & 0 & 0
\end{pmatrix}.$$

The rank-4 approximation $(\tilde{A}_4)$ computed using the QR factorization is

$$\begin{pmatrix}
0 & 0.5774 & 0 & 0.4472 & 0.5983 & 0 & 0.5983 \\
0 & 0.5774 & 0.5774 & 0 & 0.0544 & 0 & 0.0544 \\
0 & 0 & 0 & 0 & 0 & 0 & 0 \\
0 & 0 & 0 & 0.4472 & 0.2176 & 0 & 0.2176 \\
0 & 0.5774 & 0.5774 & 0 & 0.0544 & 0 & 0.0544 \\
0.7071 & 0 & 0 & 0.4472 & 0 & 0 & 0 \\
0 & 0 & 0 & 0 & 0 & 0 & 0 \\
0 & 0 & 0.5774 & 0.4472 & -0.1088 & 0 & -0.1088 \\
0.7071 & 0 & 0 & 0.4472 & 0 & 0 & 0
\end{pmatrix},$$

and the rank-4 approximation (A_4) via the SVD is

$$\begin{pmatrix}
-0.0018 & 0.5958 & -0.0148 & 0.4523 & 0.6974 & 0.0102 & 0.6974 \\
-0.0723 & 0.4938 & 0.6254 & 0.0743 & 0.0121 & -0.0133 & 0.0121 \\
0.0002 & -0.0067 & 0.0052 & -0.0013 & 0.3569 & 0.7036 & 0.3569 \\
\mathbf{0.1968} & 0.0512 & 0.0064 & 0.2179 & 0.0532 & -0.0540 & 0.0532 \\
-0.0723 & 0.4938 & 0.6254 & 0.0743 & 0.0121 & -0.0133 & 0.0121 \\
0.6315 & -0.0598 & 0.0288 & 0.5291 & -0.0008 & 0.0002 & -0.0008 \\
0.0002 & -0.0067 & 0.0052 & -0.0013 & 0.3569 & 0.7036 & 0.3569 \\
\mathbf{0.2151} & 0.2483 & 0.4347 & 0.2262 & -0.0359 & 0.0394 & -0.0359 \\
0.6315 & -0.0598 & 0.0288 & 0.5291 & -0.0008 & 0.0002 & -0.0008
\end{pmatrix}.$$

Figure 4.2: The term-by-document matrix A and its two rank-4 approximations $(A_4, \tilde{A}_4)$.

Similar to equation (4.5), the cosines of the angles between the query vector q and the n document vectors (or columns) of A_k can be represented by

$$\cos\theta_j = \frac{(A_k e_j)^T q}{\|A_k e_j\|_2 \, \|q\|_2} = \frac{(U_k \Sigma_k V_k^T e_j)^T q}{\|U_k \Sigma_k V_k^T e_j\|_2 \, \|q\|_2} \tag{4.8}$$

$$= \frac{e_j^T V_k \Sigma_k (U_k^T q)}{\|\Sigma_k V_k^T e_j\|_2 \, \|q\|_2} \quad \text{for } j = 1, 2, \ldots, n.$$

For the *scaled* document vector $s_j = \Sigma_k V_k^T e_j$, the formula in equation (4.8) can be simplified to

$$\cos\theta_j = \frac{s_j^T (U_k^T q)}{\|s_j\|_2 \, \|q\|_2}, \quad j = 1, 2, \ldots, n. \tag{4.9}$$

This implies that one need not explicitly form the rank-k matrix A_k from its SVD factors (U_k, Σ_k, V_k) and that the norms $\|s_j\|_2$ can be computed once, stored, and retrieved for all query processing.

The k elements of the vector s_j are the coordinates of the jth column of A_k in the basis defined by the columns of U_k. In addition, the k elements of the vector $U_k^T q$ are the coordinates in that basis of the projection $U_k U_k^T q$ of the query vector q into the column space of A_k [7]. An alternate formula for the cosine computation in equation (4.9) is

$$\cos\hat{\theta}_j = \frac{s_j^T (U_k^T q)}{\|s_j\|_2 \, \|U_k^T q\|_2}, \quad j = 1, 2, \ldots, n, \tag{4.10}$$

where the cost of computing the projected query vector $U_k^T q$ is usually minimal (i.e., q is typically sparse if the user supplies only a few search terms). For all document vectors (s_j), $\cos\hat{\theta}_j \geq \cos\theta_j$ so that a few more relevant documents may sometimes be retrieved if equation (4.10) rather than equation (4.9) is used.

4.2.3   Software

In order to compute the SVD of sparse term-by-document matrices, it is important to store and use only the nonzero elements of the matrix (see Section 3.2.2). Numerical methods for computing the SVD of a sparse matrix include iterative methods such as Arnoldi [56], Lanczos [47, 67], subspace iteration [67, 70], and trace minimization [74]. All of these methods reference the sparse matrix A only through matrix-vector multiplication operations, and all can be implemented in terms of the sparse storage formats discussed in Section 3.2.2. Chapter 9 provides several references and websites that provide both algorithms and software for computing the SVD of sparse matrices.

For relatively small term-by-document matrices, one may be able to ignore sparsity altogether and consider the matrix A as *dense*. The LAPACK [1] Fortran library provides portable and robust routines for computing the SVD of dense matrices. MATLAB [60] provides the dense SVD function [U,Sigma,V]=svd(A) if A is stored as a dense matrix and [U,Sigma,V]= svd(full(A)) if A is stored as a sparse matrix. MATLAB (Version 5.1) also provides a function to compute a few of the largest singular values and corresponding singular vectors of a sparse matrix. If the k largest singular values and corresponding left and right singular vectors are required, the MATLAB command [Uk,Sigmak,Vk] = svds(A,k) can be used. The sparse SVD function svds is based on the Arnoldi methods described in [55]. Less expensive factorizations such as QR (Section 4.1) and the ULV decomposition [12] can be alternatives to the SVD, whether A is dense or sparse.

4.3   Semidiscrete Decomposition

As discussed in [7], no genuine effort has been made to preserve sparsity in the reduced-rank approximation of term-by-document matrices. Since the singular vector matrices are often dense, the storage requirements for U_k, Σ_k, and V_k can vastly exceed those of the original term-by-document matrix. Semidiscrete decomposition (SDD) [43] provides one means of reducing the storage requirements of IR models such as LSI. In SDD, only the three values $\{-1, 0, 1\}$ (represented by two bits each) are used to define the elements of U_k and V_k, and a sequence of integer programming problems are solved to produce the decomposition. These mixed integer programming problems with solutions (triplets) of the form $\{\sigma_k, u_k, v_k\}$ can be represented by

$$\min_{\substack{u \in \mathcal{S}^m \\ v \in \mathcal{S}^n \\ \sigma > 0}} F_k(\sigma, u, v) \equiv \|R_k - \sigma u v^T\|_F^2, \tag{4.11}$$

where $\mathcal{S}^j$ denotes the j-dimensional subspace spanned by vectors whose components are in the set $\{-1, 0, 1\}$, $R_k = A - A_{k-1}$, and $A_0 \equiv 0$. As discussed in [43], the storage economization achieved by the SDD can result in almost a 100% reduction in memory required by the term (U_k) and document (V_k) vectors at the cost of a much larger (sometimes as much as 50%) rank (k) and subsequent computational time.

4.4 Updating Techniques

Unfortunately, once you have created an index using a matrix decomposition such as the SVD (or SDD) it will probably be obsolete in a matter of seconds. Dynamic collections (e.g., webpages) mandate the constant inclusion (or perhaps deletion) of new information. For vector space IR models based on the SVD (e.g., LSI), one approach to accommodate additions (new terms or documents) is to recompute the SVD of the new term-by-document matrix, but, for large collections, this process can be very costly in both time and space (i.e., memory). More tractable approaches such as folding-in, SVD-updating, and SDD-updating are well documented [7, 8, 43, 66, 77]. The procedure referred to as *folding-in* is fairly inexpensive computationally but typically produces an inexact representation of the updated collection. It is generally appropriate to *fold-in* only a few documents (or terms) at a time. Updating, while more expensive, preserves (or restores) the representation of the collection as if the SVD (or similar decomposition) had been recomputed. We will briefly review the folding-in procedure in light of our discussion on query matching in Section 4.2.2 and provide further (comprehensive) reading material on updating the decompositions of sparse term-by-document matrices in Chapter 9.

Folding a new document vector into the column space of an existing term-by-document is synonymous with finding the coordinates for that document in an existing basis (U_k). To fold a new $m \times 1$ document vector $\hat{p}$ into the (k-dimensional) column space of an $m \times n$ term-by-document matrix A means to *project* $\hat{p}$ onto that space [7]. If p represents the projection of $\hat{p}$, then it follows (see Section 4.2.2) that

$$p = U_k U_k^T \hat{p}.$$

Hence, the coordinates (k of them) for p in the basis U_k are determined by the elements of $U_k^T \hat{p}$.

The new document is then *folded-in* by appending (as a new column) the k-dimensional vector $U_k^T \hat{p}$ to the existing $k \times n$ matrix $\Sigma_k V_k^T$, where n is the number of previously indexed documents. In the event that the matrix product $\Sigma_k V_k^T$ is not explicitly computed, we can simply append $\hat{p}^T U_k \Sigma_k^{-1}$ as a new row of V_k to form a new matrix $\hat{V}_k$. The product $\Sigma_k \hat{V}_k$ is the desired result, and we note that the matrix $\hat{V}_k$ is no longer orthonormal. In fact, the row space of the matrix $\hat{V}_k^T$ does not represent the row space of the new term-by-document matrix. In the event that the new document vector $\hat{p}$ is *nearly* orthogonal to the columns of U_k, most information about that document is lost in the projection p. From Section 3.2.3, we illustrate the folding-in of the new document

D8: Safety Guide for Child Proofing Your Home

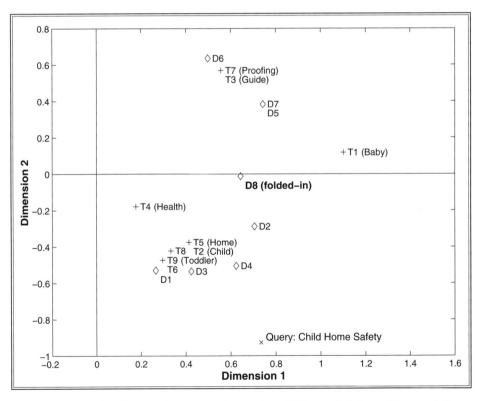

Figure 4.3: Folding-in D8 into the rank-2 LSI model from Figure 3.3.

into the rank-2 (SVD-based) approximation of the 9×7 term-by-document matrix A in Figure 3.1. For D8, we define

$$\hat{p} = q/\|q\|_2 \text{ for } q = (\,0 \quad 1 \quad 1 \quad 0 \quad 1 \quad 0 \quad 1 \quad 1 \quad 0\,)^T,$$

so that

$$\hat{p} = (\,0 \quad 0.4472 \quad 0.4472 \quad 0 \quad 0.4472 \quad 0 \quad 0.4472 \quad 0.4472 \quad 0\,)^T.$$

The two coordinates for the projected document (p) are defined by

$$p = U_2^T \hat{p} = (\,0.6439 \quad -0.0128\,)^T,$$

where the rank-2 SVD-based IR model is $A_2 = U_2 \Sigma_2 V_2^T$. Figure 4.3 illustrates the projection[5] of D8 into the same 2-dimensional vector space depicted in Figure 3.3.

To fold-in an $n \times 1$ term vector $\hat{w}$ whose elements specify the documents associated with a term, $\hat{w}$ is projected into the row space of A_k. If w represents the term projection of $\hat{w}$, then

$$w = V_k V_k^T \hat{w}.$$

The k coordinates $V_k^T \hat{w}$ of the projected vector w are then appended (as a new row) to the matrix U_k. In this case, we lose orthogonality in our k-dimensional basis for the column space of A (see [8, 66] for further details).

---

[5]Similar to the comment in Section 3.2.3, an equivalent (mirrored) plot would have the coordinates of D8 as $(-0.6439, 0.0128)$.

Chapter 5

Query Management

Although a good portion of this book has been focused on the use of vector space IR models (e.g., LSI), it is important to continually remind ourselves and readers alike that there are several proven approaches used to build search engines. Other indexing models have certain strengths and limitations, and this becomes evident when one looks at query management, or the process of translating the user's query into a form that the search engine can utilize. The relationship between the system and the query has a catch-22 flavor. Selecting the most efficient search engine may depend on the type of query allowed, which in turn depends on the indexing model used by a search engine.

In other words, certain types of search engine models handle certain types of queries better, but the user may have some other type of query in mind altogether. In this chapter, the focus will be on general guidelines for query management along with some discussion on the effects query types and search engines can have on each other.

5.1 Query Binding

Query binding is a general term describing the three-tier process of translating the user's need into a search engine query. The first level involves the user formulating the information need into a question or a list of terms using his or her own experiences and vocabulary and entering it into the search engine. On the next level, the search engine must translate the words (with possible spelling errors such as cran*beery*) into processing tokens (as discussed in Section 2.4). Finally, on the third level, the search engine must use the processing tokens to search the document database and retrieve the appropriate documents (see Figure 5.1).

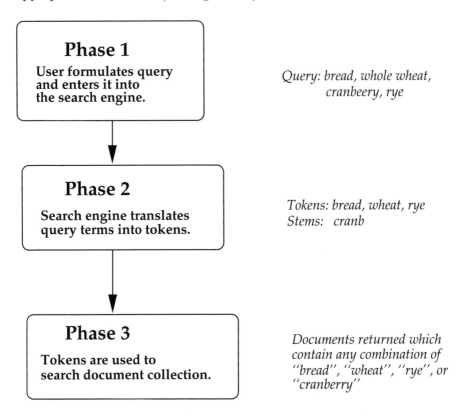

Figure 5.1: Three phases of query binding.

In practice, users (based on their work experience and skill level) may enter their query in a variety of different ways: as a Boolean statement, as a question (*natural language* query), as a list of terms with proximity operators and contiguous word phrases, or with the use of a thesaurus. Problems therefore arise when search engines cannot accept all types of queries [18]. A query that uses a Boolean operator such as *AND* or *OR* has to be processed differently than a natural language query. Building a search engine to accept a certain type of query ultimately forces the user to *learn* how to enter queries in that manner.

This is not to say that one type of query is better than another but rather to point out that there are several types of queries, and search engine design is extremely dependent on what type of queries the search engine will accept. Part of choosing the type of query is also dependent on anticipating who will be using the search engine. A beginning or inexperienced searcher such as a high school student will probably be more comfortable with a natural language query, whereas an information professional who is familiar with advanced search features will be more comfortable with a system that can perform Boolean searches or searches using proximity parameters and contiguous word phrases.

5.2 Types of Queries

There are several types of queries. Each type should be evaluated with respect to how the user enters it and what he or she expects in return, its strengths and limitations, and compatibility with the search engine design. There are no hard and fast rules when discussing query/search engine compatibility. It is also interesting to note that the current trend for most operational systems is to apply a combination of queries with the hope that users will learn the best strategies to use for a given system [58]. Some systems are more *hybrid* than others and offer information seekers choices between exact (lexical) match Boolean and ranked approaches.

5.2.1 Boolean Queries

Boolean logic queries link words in the search using operators such as *AND*, *OR*, and *NOT*. Recall the document file in Section 2.5 (the Bread Search limerick). If the searcher wanted the document which contains the words *meat OR wheat*, documents three, six, and seven would be pulled, but if the searcher wanted *meat AND wheat*, no documents would have been pulled. Why? Because none of the lines of the limerick contain both words *meat* and *wheat*. (To keep your Boolean operators straight remember the adage, "*OR* gets you more.") The *NOT* operator is more troublesome, because it forces the system to exclude members from the pulled or returned set of results. One of the weaknesses of Boolean queries, according to [44], is that there does not appear to be a good way to gauge significance in a Boolean query.

Either a term is present or it is absent. Current research [44] suggests that most users of information systems are not well trained in Boolean operators (unlike computer scientists and mathematicians). For systems based on a vector space IR model, Boolean operators are typically recognized as stop words, and hence are ignored.

5.2.2   Natural Language Queries

Natural language queries (NLQs) are queries in which the user formulates as a question or a statement. Using the Bread Search limerick from Section 2.5, a viable NLQ might be

> Which documents have information on manna?

or

> Where is information on the use of manna as a connotation for spirituality?

To process an NLQ, the search engine must extract all indexed terms to initiate a search. Obviously, some words in the query will be eliminated by the use of stop lists. This approach, according to Korfhage in [44], has the distinct disadvantage in that

> "...computers have difficulty extracting a term with its syntactic, semantic and pragmatic knowledge intact."

In other words, once you extract a word from an NLQ, the *context* of how that word is used becomes lost.

For example, in the NLQ once the word *manna* is removed from the query, then the system does not know whether the meaning is *manna for bread* or *manna for spiritual sustenance*. This is not a major concern perhaps in the case of *manna*, but when a word can have multiple and varied meanings (i.e., when it is polysemous), then the effect can be much more pronounced.

5.2.3   Thesaurus Queries

A *thesaurus query* is one where the user selects the term from a previous set of terms predetermined by the IR system. The advantage of the thesaurus query is that the first phase of query binding (see Figure 5.1) is automated for the user. Also, thesauri can readily expand to related concepts. On the other hand, the searcher is bound to the thesaurus term even if he or she does not think the term is the *best* choice. Furthermore, there can be problems with understanding the specific meaning of a word. For example, in the Bread Search limerick, if the user is using the thesaurus to search on the spiritual aspects of *manna*, the system may only consider manna as bread described in the Old Testament of the Bible.

As mentioned by Kowalski in [45], thesauri tend to be generic to a language and can thus introduce/insert many search terms that were never indexed or found in the collection. This is less of a problem in an IR system where the thesaurus has been especially built for the database; however, the costs to do so may be prohibitive.

5.2.4 Fuzzy Queries

It seems appropriate that the concept of *fuzzy searches* is somewhat *fuzzy* itself. Fuzzy reflects nonspecificity and can be viewed in two ways. As described in [45], fuzziness in a search system refers to the capability of handling the misspelling or variations of the same words. User queries are automatically stemmed, and documents related to (or containing) the word stems are retrieved. Using the Bread Search document collection from Section 2.5, a fuzzy query, which misspelled the word *cranberry* as *cranbeery*, would still (hopefully) return documents on cranberries, as the word stem (root) *cranb* would be the same for both words.

Fuzzy queries can also be viewed in terms of the sets of retrieved documents. It is similar to standard retrieval systems in which the retrieved documents are returned by order of relevancy. However, in the fuzzy retrieval system the threshold of relevancy is expanded to include additional documents, which may be of interest to the user (see [44]).

5.2.5 Term Searches

Perhaps the most prevalent type of query (especially on the Web) is when a user provides a few words or phrases for the search. More experienced searchers might prefer using a *contiguous* word phrase such as *Atlanta Falcons* to find information about that football team. Otherwise, if the search engine does not interpret the query as a phrase, documents about the city of *Atlanta* or documents about *birds* would more than likely be erroneously retrieved. The use of contiguous phrases improves the chance of precision (see Section 6.1.1) at the risk of losing a few documents that might have been selected. For example, if an article read,

> In Atlanta, the Falcons host their arch rivals...

it would not be retrieved (lower recall). In the next chapter on ranking and relevance feedback, the issues of precision and recall will be discussed further.

On the other hand, the experienced searcher may use a *proximity* operator, i.e., designate to the system that he or she wants a document that has the words *Atlanta* and *Falcons* with fewer than five words between them. (In most systems, users can choose five words, ten words, and so on).

As mentioned in Section 2.5, in order for systems to support proximity operators and contiguous phrases, the inversion list must track not only which terms appear in which documents but also the position of those terms in the documents. This certainly requires more storage and processing capabilities.

One interesting dilemma for the user is deciding how many terms to supply. Users have a tendency to type in just two or three terms. This would be fine if the system was more match-oriented or based on the Boolean *OR* operator. However, if the IR system is based on a vector space model, the user may have more success with more terms. In this context, more terms means more vectors to synthesize and construct the final query vector. However, the user may not realize that the query (in this case) could be more of a *pseudodocument* representation for conceptual matching, as opposed to a long string of terms for lexical matching (see [7, 8, 25]).

5.2.6 Probabilistic Queries

Probabilistic queries refer to the manner in which the IR system retrieves documents according to relevancy. The premise for this type of search is that for a given document and a query it should be possible to compute a probability of relevancy for the document with respect to the query. In [44], the difference between Boolean- and vector-based matching and probabilistic matching is summarized as follows:

> "One concern about both Boolean- and vector-based matching is that they are based on *hard* criteria. In Boolean-based matching,

either a document meets the logical conditions or it does not; in vector-based matching, a similarity threshold is set, and either a document falls above that threshold or it does not. The ability to define various similarity measures and thresholds in the vector case softens the impact of the threshold value to some extent. However, a number of researchers, believing that even this does not adequately represent the uncertainties that abound in text retrieval, focus their attention on models that include uncertainties more directly."

Marchionini in [58] acknowledges that in probabilistic IR modeling there are degrees (or levels) of relevance that can be based on some estimated probability of document-query relevance. One advantage of probabilistic queries over fuzzy queries is that there is a well-established body of methods for computing probabilities from frequency data [44]. For additional reading on probabilistic IR models (theory and empirical testing), we refer the reader to [19, 52].

Chapter 6

Ranking and Relevance Feedback

Even though at first it seems that all search engines have the same basic features, one aspect that separates more full, functional search engines from their lesser counterparts is the ability not only to list the search results in a meaningful way (ranking) but also to allow the user a chance of using those results to resubmit another, more on-target query. This latter feature, referred to as *relevance feedback*, has been quite effective in helping users find more relevant documents with less effort [72]. Harman [36] has done extensive work in judging how relevance feedback positively affects system performance.

Marchionini [58] points out another advantage of ranking and relevance feedback. As computer designers continue in their quest to make computers more receptive to users, ranking and relevance feedback can be considered as *highly interactive* information seeking. Along the same vein, Korfhage [44] refers to relevance feedback as a type of *dialogue* between user and system.

Some commercial systems limit this feature and elect to forego building it into the system since relevance feedback can create computational burdens that can slow a system down. Also, it requires constant updating of the system's knowledge of itself because in order for the search engine to know if a certain document is the best it must know what every document in the system contains. By using applied mathematics, producing a rank-ordered list of documents, and relevance feedback, search engine performance can be improved. Subsequently, vector space IR models such as LSI (see Chapter 3) can be more readily adapted to providing relevance feedback. According to Marchionini,

> "The vector approach has a significant advantage over traditional indexing methods for end users, because the retrieved sets of documents can be ranked, thus eliminating the *no hits* result so common in exact-match systems. Experimental systems that provide ranked output have proved highly effective and commercial vendors have begun to offer ranked output features. Ranked output also provides a reasonable entry point for browsing." [58]

6.1   Performance Evaluation

A variation of the sometimes pointless adage,

> "It doesn't matter whether you win or lose, it's how you play the game,"

is applicable in evaluating the performance of search engines. In one aspect, the ultimate evaluation of any search system is determined by whether the user is satisfied with results of the search. In short, has the information need been met in a timely manner? If so, the system and the user alike are declared the winner.

But this kind of simplistic thinking is, well, too simplistic. User satisfaction can certainly be measured in a variety of ways: *binary* (i.e., the results are acceptable or unacceptable) or *relative* (e.g., ranks a 5 on a scale of 1 to 10 with 10 being perfect). Also, other considerations need to be addressed when evaluating a system, such as whether the user did not get the desired results because of a poor query in the first place. A misspelled word, the need for quotation marks to be added to a phrase, or lack of understanding of exactly what needs to be asked can also affect a search engine's performance.

Korfhage [44] also points out that users will not tolerate more than three or four attempts of feeding back information to the system, nor does the user like seeing the same set of documents appearing over and over again. This brings out an interesting dilemma for the system designer. For example, after receiving a list of documents, suppose the user marks a certain document as *retrieve more like this one*. In the new return list of results, should that document be automatically at the top of the next list even though conceivably it could be ranked lower than the new set of documents? Then again, if the document is not at the top of the list, the user may wonder why.

Such problems, however, have not prevented researchers from developing some standards for at least discussing and comparing the results of a search, whether it be searching on the Web, an on-line database, or a CD-ROM.

6.1.1 Precision

Unlike information science professionals who are drilled early on in their academic careers by the standard definitions of precision and recall, system designers may not be as familiar with the terms and the implications of their use. This is understandable because it is one thing to design and build a system, and it is another thing to evaluate it. *Precision* and *recall* are two of the standard definitions used in search system evaluation, and because they are so closely related they are usually discussed in tandem.

The precision or precision ratio P of a search method is defined as

$$P = \frac{D_r}{D_t}, \tag{6.1}$$

where D_r is the number of relevant documents retrieved and D_t is the total number of documents retrieved. It is important to keep in mind that *relevance*, or the appropriateness of a document to a user's needs, is still a judgment call. Two searchers can be looking for the same information in the same topic, and when the results are listed, *Article* 4 may strike *searcher A* as useful or relevant, whereas *searcher B* may find *Article* 4 to be irrelevant and not useful. Relevance is subjective and dependent on who is keeping score. Sometimes it is the end user. Sometimes it is an intermediator (an information broker, for example) who is making that determination for someone else, and sometimes it is a disinterested third party system evaluator who is simply evaluating search engines (and has no vested interest in the information itself).

6.1.2 Recall

The recall or recall ratio R of a search method is defined as

$$R = \frac{D_r}{N_r}, \tag{6.2}$$

where D_r is the same numerator from equation (6.1) and N_r is the total number of relevant documents in the collection. Recall ratios are somewhat difficult to obtain, as the *total* number of relevant documents is always an unknown. In other words, how does one compute the recall ratio if he or she is not really sure how many relevant documents are in the collection in the first place? However, that does not lessen the usefulness of the recall ratio.

In one sense, precision and recall are on a continuum. If a searcher wants only the precise documents that fits his or her exact needs, then the query will require very specific terms. However, there is the danger or trade-off that if the search is extremely precise, many relevant documents will be missed. That explains the integral role of recall. The search must be broadened so that a significant number of relevant documents will be included in the results of the search. Again there is a another trade-off: if the recall is increased, the user more than likely will have to wade through what is known as *false drops, garbage*, and *noise* to pick out the relevant documents. What a user generally needs is a complete subset of relevant documents that does not require a substantial *weeding out* of all the irrelevant material.

6.1.3   Average Precision

Average precision is a common measure used in the IR community to assess retrieval performance [35]. Let r_i denote the number of relevant documents up to and including position i in the (ordered) returned list of documents. The recall at the ith document in the list (the first document is assumed to be most relevant) is the proportion of relevant documents *seen* thus far, i.e., $R_i = r_i/r_n$. The precision at the ith document, P_i, is defined to be the proportion of documents up to including position i that are relevant to the given query. Hence, $P_i = r_i/i$. The so-called *pseudoprecision* at a recall level x is then defined by

$$\tilde{P}(x) = \max P_i, \text{where } x \le \frac{r_i}{r_n}, \text{ and } i = 1, 2, \dots, n. \tag{6.3}$$

Using equation (6.3), the n-point (interpolated) *average precision* for a query is given by

$$P_{av} = \frac{1}{n} \sum_{i=0}^{n-1} \tilde{P}\left(\frac{i}{n-1}\right).$$

As it is common to observe retrieval at recall levels $k/10$, for $k = 0, 1, \dots, 10$, an $n = 11$ point average precision (P_{av}) is typically used to measure the performance of an IR system for each query. If a single measure is desired for multiple queries, the mean (or median) P_{av} across all queries can be recorded.

6.1.4 Genetic Algorithms

Genetic algorithms can be used in conjunction with relevance feedback calculations to monitor several relevance feedback scenarios simultaneously before choosing the best one. The premise with this *combined* approach is that in the normal relevance feedback situation the user makes a decision early on, and many documents are quickly discarded. However, some of those discards could be relevant or lead to relevant documents, so in a system using a genetic algorithm those discarded documents are used to create *alternate paths* to run in parallel to the main set of queries. Later on, the system will determine whether the alternative sets of documents merit further consideration. Korfhage has done extensive work in genetic algorithms and has dedicated several sections of his book [44] to this topic.

6.2 Relevance Feedback

An *ideal* IR system would achieve high precision for all levels of recall. That is, it would identify all relevant documents without returning any irrelevant ones. Unfortunately, due to problems such as polysemy and synonymy (see Chapter 3), a list of documents retrieved for a given query is hardly perfect, and the user has to discern which items to keep/read and which ones to discard.

Salton in [72] and Harman in [36] have demonstrated that precision can be improved using *relevance feedback*, i.e., specifying which documents from a returned set are most relevant so that those documents can be used to refine/clarify the original query. Relevance feedback can be implemented using the column space of the term-by-document matrix A (see Section 3.1.2). More specifically, the query can be replaced or modified by the vector sum of the most relevant (user-judged) documents returned in order to focus the search *closer* to those document vectors.

We will assume that the original query vector (q) lies within the column space of the matrix A_k, the low-rank approximation to the term-by-document matrix A (see Sections 3.2.3 and 4.2). Otherwise, the query vector is replaced by its projection onto that column space ($U_k U_k^T q$ for

SVD-encoded collections). For convenience, both query and document vectors can be represented using the same basis for the rank-k approximation to the column space of A [7]. For SVD-based approximations (Section 4.2), this basis is determined by the columns of U_k, where $A_k = U_k \Sigma_k V_k^T$. The coordinates of the query vector are simply the elements of the vector $U_k^T q$, and the coordinates of the jth column $U_k \Sigma_k V_k^T e_j$ of the matrix A_k are the elements of the vector $\Sigma_k V_k^T e_j$.

If a user considered, say, the tenth document (a_{10}) of a collection to be most relevant for his or her search, then the new query q_{new} (based on relevance feedback) can be represented as

$$
\begin{aligned}
q_{new} &= U_k U_k^T q + a_{10} \\
&= U_k U_k^T q + U_k \Sigma_k V_k^T e_{10} \\
&= U_k (U_k^T q + \Sigma_k V_k^T e_{10}).
\end{aligned} \tag{6.4}
$$

If the user judges a larger set of documents to be relevant, the new/modified query can be written as

$$
q_{new} = q + \sum_{j=1}^{d} w_j a_j = U_k (U_k^T q + \Sigma_k V_k^T w), \tag{6.5}
$$

where the vector element w_j is 1 if a_j is relevant and 0 otherwise. If the user (or the IR system) desires to replace the original query by a sum of document vectors, the vector q in equation (6.5) is simply set to 0.

Note that the vector $U_k^T q$ in equations (6.4) and (6.5) can be formed in the original cosine computation with the original query vector q. Hence, the new query (q_{new}) can be determined efficiently via the sum of k-dimensional vectors and then compared with all documents vectors. Following equation (4.9), we can define the vector $s_j = \Sigma_k V_k^T e_j$ so that the appropriate cosine formula becomes

$$
\cos \theta_j = \frac{s_j^T (U_k^T q_{new})}{\| s_j \|_2 \| q_{new} \|_2}
$$

for $j = 1, 2, \ldots, n$. As was shown in [27], experiments have shown that replacing a query with a combination of a few of the most relevant documents to the query returned can significantly improve the precision of LSI for some collections.

Chapter 7

Searching by Link Structure

The most dramatic change in search engine design in the past several years has been developing search engines that account for the Web's hyperlink structure. LSI, with its SVD of a term-by-document matrix, is an approach that works well for smaller document collections but has problems with scalability. The computation and storage of an SVD-based LSI model for the entire Web is not tractable [49].

In general, the idea of this relatively new approach is that there are certain pages on the Web that are recognized as the "go to" places for certain information, and there is another set of pages that legitimize those esteemed positions by pointing to them with links. For example, let us say there is a website called *The History of Meat and Potatoes*. If enough other websites link to *The History of Meat and Potatoes* website, then *The History of Meat and Potatoes* shows up high on the list when queries are made. These "go to" places are known as *authorities*, and those webpages that point to authorities are known as *hubs*. It is a mutually reinforcing approach, with good hubs pointing to good authorities and good authorities pointing to good hubs [46].

In 1998, Jon Kleinberg of Cornell University formalized this approach with the hyperlink induced topic search (HITS) algorithm, which takes into account the Web's social network. Basically, not only does the query pull in a set of pages that matches the term, but it also evaluates webpages that link to the term. Ultimately, the user is presented with both sets of pages — the authoritative and the hub list. This is explained in more detail in Section 7.1.1. One example of how those results might appear on the screen is found at the website for the search engine Teoma (`www.teoma.com`). Teoma provides the user not only with a standard results lists but also a list of additional "authorities."

The advantage of the HITS algorithm for web queries is that the user receives two lists of results: a set of authoritative pages he or she seeks and a set of link pages that can give a more comprehensive look at the information that is available. One major disadvantage is that these computations are made after the query is made, so the time to create the lists would be unacceptable to most users. Also, on the downside, a webmaster can skew the results by adding links to one's own page to increase the authority score and hub score [49].

Another more well-known, similar, linkage data approach is the PageRank algorithm developed by the founders of Google, Larry Page and Sergey Brin [49]. Page and Brin were graduate students at Stanford in 1998 when they published a paper describing the fundamental concepts of the PageRank algorithm, which later was used as the underlying algorithm that currently drives Google [49]. Unlike the HITS algorithm, where the results are created after the query is made, Google has the Web crawled and indexed ahead of time, and the links within these pages are analyzed before the query is ever entered by the user. Basically, Google looks not only at the number of links to *The History of Meat and Potatoes* website — referring to the earlier example — but also the importance of those referring links. Google determines how many other Meat and Potatoes websites are also being linked to the referring site and what is important about those sites. Again, all of this is computed before the query is ever typed by the user. Once a query comes, the results are returned based on these intricate PageRank values.

Although the Google search engine is in a dominant position in the web searching marketplace, it is not without its shortcomings. A strategy to improve one's position on a results page known as "Googlebombing" involves creating additional websites or manipulating weblogs (knowns as "blogs") that can beef up the number of referring links artificially [85, 37]. Like most of the major commercial search engines, Google is limited in its advanced concept matching [85]. Referring to the earlier *Meat and Potatoes* example, if a user queries with synonyms such as "beef," "spuds," and "history," the chances of a results list with *The History of Meat and Potatoes* as one the top entries would be less likely. Also, if the user wanted to know about *The History of Meat and Potatoes in China*, it would be difficult to process the polysemic query term "China." Would the search engine process the term "China" as meaning China as an Asian country or china meaning "fine dishes"? See [42].

It is important to note that the HITS and the PageRank algorithms are not the only approaches that take into account the hyperlink structure of the Web. Other methods such as the stochastic approach for link structure analysis (SALSA) algorithm of Lempel and Moran combine elements of the HITS and PageRank algorithms [49]. However, in the remaining sections of this chapter, the focus shifts to the theoretical aspects of the two original link algorithms, HITS and PageRank.

7.1 HITS Method

Recall that the premise of the HITS method for modeling link structure assumes that *good* authorities are pointed to by *good* hubs and good hubs point to good authorities. Let us suppose that webpage i has an authority score a_i and hub score h_i. Also, let $\mathcal{E}$ denote the set of all directed edges in a graph of the Web whereby e_{ij} represents the directed edge from node (or webpage) i to node j. If we assume that every webpage has been assigned an initial authority score $a_i^{(0)}$ and hub score $h_i^{(0)}$, the HITS method iteratively updates these scores by the following summations:

$$a_i^{(k)} = \sum_j h_j^{(k-1)}, \text{ where } e_{ji} \in \mathcal{E},$$

$$h_i^{(k)} = \sum_j a_j^{(k-1)}, \text{ where } e_{ij} \in \mathcal{E}, \tag{7.1}$$

for $k = 1, 2, 3, \ldots$. As discussed in [49], the above equations can be recast in matrix notation using the adjacency matrix L (of the directed web graph) defined by

$$L_{ij} = \begin{cases} 1 & \text{if there exists } i \text{ and } j \text{ such that } e_{ij} \in \mathcal{E}, \\ 0 & \text{otherwise.} \end{cases}$$

For the 5-node web graph depicted in Figure 7.1, the 5×5 adjacency matrix L is given by

$$L = \begin{pmatrix} 0 & 0 & 1 & 0 & 1 \\ 1 & 0 & 1 & 0 & 0 \\ 0 & 1 & 0 & 1 & 0 \\ 1 & 0 & 0 & 0 & 1 \\ 0 & 0 & 1 & 0 & 0 \end{pmatrix}.$$

Notice that the summations in equation (7.1) can be rewritten as the matrix-vector multiplications

$$\vec{a}^{(k)} = L^T \vec{h}^{(k-1)} \text{ and } \vec{h}^{(k)} = L\vec{a}^{(k)}, \qquad (7.2)$$

where $\vec{a}^{(k)}$ and $\vec{h}^{(k)}$ are $n \times 1$ vectors comprising the authority and hub scores, respectively, for each of the n nodes (webpages) in the graph. The final (or converged) authority and hub scores in $\vec{a}$ and $\vec{h}$ can be obtained by repeatedly updating equation (7.2) until $\vec{a}^{(k)}$ and $\vec{h}^{(k)}$ converge for some k. Typically, $\vec{a}^{(k)}$ and $\vec{h}^{(k)}$ are normalized after each update (iteration k) [49]. By a few simple substitutions, the HITS iteration can be written as

$$\vec{a}^{(k)} = L^T L \vec{a}^{(k-1)} \text{ and } \vec{h}^{(k)} = L L^T \vec{h}^{(k-1)}. \qquad (7.3)$$

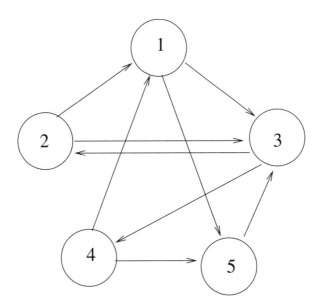

Figure 7.1: 5-node web graph.

The iterations defined by equation (7.3) are essentially the steps of the power method [33] for computing the dominant eigenvectors of $L^T L$ and LL^T. The matrix $L^T L$ can be thought of as the *authority matrix* since it is used to derive the final authority scores. Similarly, the matrix LL^T can be considered the *hub matrix*, as its dominant eigenvector will yield the final hub scores.[6] Noting that both the authority and hub matrices are positive semidefinite, the computation of $\vec{a}$ and $\vec{h}$ amounts to solving the eigensystems

$$L^T L \, \vec{a} = \lambda_{max} \, \vec{a} \text{ and } LL^T \, \vec{h} = \lambda_{max} \, \vec{h},$$

where λ_{max} is the largest eigenvalue of $L^T L$ (which is also the largest eigenvalue of LL^T). As discussed in [61], each power iteration involving $\vec{a}^{(k)}$ or $\vec{h}^{(k)}$ should be suitably normalized to guarantee convergence to the dominant eigenvalue of $L^T L$ or LL^T, respectively. Possible normalizations (see [49]) are

$$\vec{a}^{(k)} \leftarrow \frac{\vec{a}^{(k)}}{m(\vec{a}^{(k)})} \text{ and } \vec{h}^{(k)} \leftarrow \frac{\vec{h}^{(k)}}{m(\vec{h}^{(k)})},$$

where $m(\vec{x})$ is the (signed) element of maximal magnitude of $\vec{x}$.

7.1.1 HITS Implementation

To perform query matching using HITS, one must first construct a *neighborhood graph* $\mathcal{N}$ associated with a user's query terms. The authority and hub scores for the documents (or nodes) in $\mathcal{N}$ are then computed as described in equation (7.3) and returned (along with document links) to the user. One simple way to construct $\mathcal{N}$ is to use an inverted list similar to the one shown in Table 2.4 in Section 2.5.3. Using the limerick example, the query *meat with potato and wheat* would yield an initial graph ($\mathcal{N}$) of four nodes or documents $\{3, 4, 6, 7\}$ based on these entries of the inversion list:

Term	(Doc. No., Position)
.	.
meat	(7,6)
potato	(4,3)
.	.
wheat	(3,5); (6,6)

---

[6]A dominant eigenvector is the eigenvector which corresponds to the largest (in magnitude) eigenvalue.

The graph $\mathcal{N}$ is then expanded by adding nodes (webpages) that either point (link) to the nodes in $\mathcal{N}$ or are pointed to by the nodes in $\mathcal{N}$. This graph expansion will typically bring in related documents containing synonyms of the original query terms [49]. If a document/webpage containing several of the query terms has a large *indegree* (number of webpages that point to it) or large *outdegree* (number of webpages it points to), the resulting expanded graph could be enormous. To bound the size of $\mathcal{N}$, one can simply restrict the number of nodes (or webpages) included solely as an inlink or outlink of a webpage containing any or all query terms. This process of building a neighborhood graph for a query is very similar to the process of constructing level sets in information filtering [88].

Once the graph $\mathcal{N}$ is fully constructed for the query, the corresponding adjacency matrix L can be constructed. As discussed in Section 7.1, the computed dominant eigenvectors of $L^T L$ and LL^T yield the authority and hub scores which are then presented to the user in descending order (with the most related pages appearing first). For webpage ranking, the order of L is nowhere near the size of the Web so that HITS scoring usually incurs a relatively modest computational cost. As pointed out in [49], an additional reduction in cost can be achieved by computing only one dominant eigenvector of either $L^T L$ or LL^T and deriving the other dominant eigenvector by multiplication with L or L^T. For example, the authority vector $\vec{a}$ could be derived from the hub vector $\vec{h}$ (the dominant eigenvector of LL^T) by $\vec{a} = L^T \vec{h}$. Figure 7.2 illustrates how authority and hub rankings can be generated from the simple 5-node web graph from Figure 7.1. As there are equal scores (identical vector elements) in the final authority ($\vec{a}$) and hub ($\vec{h}$) vectors, a tie-breaking strategy [49] must be applied to produce final rankings. In this example, ties are broken according to position (index) in vector. The HITS algorithm suggests that node (webpage) 3 is a clear authority in the graph $\mathcal{N}$, while nodes 1 and 2 are suitable hubs. This is not too surprising, as node 3 clearly has more inlinks (three to be exact) than any of the other nodes. The identification of a dominant hub is not so immediate, as the set nodes $\{1, 2, 4\}$ all have the same number of outlinks.

7.1.2 HITS Summary

The ability to rank both authorities and hubs is a clear advantage of the HITS algorithm. Building adjacency matrices from the somewhat smaller neighborhood graphs (compared to the entire Web) and applying power

Suppose that the subset of nodes (webpages) containing a user's query terms are $\{1, 4\}$. From the corresponding 5-node graph $\mathcal{N}$ (see Figure 7.1), the corresponding adjacency matrix L (see Section 7.1) is defined as

$$L = \begin{pmatrix} 0 & 0 & 1 & 0 & 1 \\ 1 & 0 & 1 & 0 & 0 \\ 0 & 1 & 0 & 1 & 0 \\ 1 & 0 & 0 & 0 & 1 \\ 0 & 0 & 1 & 0 & 0 \end{pmatrix}.$$

The corresponding authority $(L^T L)$ and hub (LL^T) matrices are

$$L^T L = \begin{pmatrix} 2 & 0 & 1 & 0 & 1 \\ 0 & 1 & 0 & 1 & 0 \\ 1 & 0 & 3 & 0 & 1 \\ 0 & 1 & 0 & 1 & 0 \\ 1 & 0 & 1 & 0 & 2 \end{pmatrix} \text{ and } LL^T = \begin{pmatrix} 2 & 1 & 0 & 1 & 1 \\ 1 & 2 & 0 & 1 & 1 \\ 0 & 0 & 2 & 0 & 0 \\ 1 & 1 & 0 & 2 & 0 \\ 1 & 1 & 0 & 0 & 1 \end{pmatrix}.$$

Using the power iterations

$$\vec{a}^{(k)} \leftarrow \frac{\vec{a}^{(k)}}{\|\vec{a}^{(k)}\|_1} \text{ and } \vec{h}^{(k)} \leftarrow \frac{\vec{h}^{(k)}}{\|\vec{h}^{(k)}\|_1},$$

with $\vec{a}^{(0k)}$ and $\vec{h}^{(0k)}$ defined as 5×1 vectors of all 1's, we obtain the following authority $(\vec{a})$ and hub $(\vec{h})$ vectors:

$$\begin{aligned} \vec{a}^T &= (\,0.2929 \quad 0 \qquad 0.4142 \quad 0 \qquad 0.2929\,), \\ \vec{h}^T &= (\,0.2929 \quad 0.2929 \quad 0 \qquad 0.2426 \quad 0.1716\,). \end{aligned}$$

After sorting the authority and hub scores (vector elements) in decreasing order, the following rankings are generated:

$$\text{Authority ranking} = (\,2 \quad 4 \quad 1 \quad 5 \quad 3\,) \text{ and}$$
$$\text{Hub ranking} = (\,1 \quad 2 \quad 5 \quad 3 \quad 4\,).$$

Figure 7.2: HITS example using the 5-node graph from Figure 7.1.

iterations does not present a computational burden. The problem lies in the fact that the neighborhood graph must be built "on the fly"; i.e., the authority and hub rankings are definitely query-dependent. Minor changes (or updates) to the Web could significantly change the authority and hub scores. The interdependency of the authority ($\vec{a}$) and hub ($\vec{h}$) vectors means that changes to one could drastically affect the other. Attempts by users to thwart the rankings by augmenting the link patterns of the Web and subsequent neighborhood graph ($\mathcal{N}$) are possible. Modifications to the HITS algorithm to address such problems have been studied [14]. As mentioned in [49, 14], HITS can suffer from *topic drift* in that the neighborhood graph $\mathcal{N}$ could contain nodes (webpages) which have high authority scores for a topic unrelated to the original query. To counter this problem, vector models such as LSI (see Chapter 1) can be exploited to assess/measure the (semantic) relevance of a node or webpage to the original query terms.

7.2   PageRank Method

PageRank, the webpage scoring approach adopted by Google developers Brin and Page (see [20, 21]), produces rankings independent of a user's query. The importance of a webpage in this case is determined (in large part) by the number of other important webpages that are pointing to that page and the number of outlinks from those other webpages. Let us define the rank of a webpage P_i to be $r(P_i)$, $\mathcal{T}_{P_i}$ the set of all webpages which point to P_i, and $|Q|$ the number of outlinks from an arbitrary webpage Q. Then, $r(P_i)$ is recursively defined by

$$r_j(P_i) = \sum_{Q \in \mathcal{T}_{P_i}} \frac{r_{j-1}(Q)}{|Q|} \text{ for } j = 1, 2, 3, \ldots.$$

Alternatively, if we set $\vec{x}_j^T = (r_j(P_1), r_j(P_2), \ldots, r_j(P_n))$, then the iteration reduces to

$$\vec{x}_j^T = \vec{x}_{j-1}^T A, \tag{7.4}$$

where $A = [a_{ij}]$ is the $n \times n$ transition probability matrix of a Markov chain [61, Ch. 8], [63] defined by

$$a_{ij} = \begin{cases} 1/|P_i| & \text{if } P_i \text{ links to } P_j, \\ 0 & \text{otherwise.} \end{cases}$$

If the power iteration in equation (7.4) converges to its dominant left eigen-vector $\vec{x}$, then the ith component of the limiting vector produces the PageRank scores for all the webpages, i.e.,

$$\vec{x}_i = r(P_i) \text{ for } i = 1, 2, \ldots, n.$$

For ranking all possible webpages, the matrix A in equation (7.4) would have over four billion rows (and columns), and computing its dominant left eigenvector is certainly a formidable challenge. As discussed in [63], this may well be the largest matrix computation ever posed.

In order to guarantee that the power iteration converges to a unique (and positive) solution $\vec{x}$, commonly referred to as the *stationary distribution vector* for the corresponding Markov chain, some adjustments have to be made to the matrix A.

7.2.1 PageRank Adjustments

The matrix A from equation (7.4), also referred to as the raw hyperlinked matrix [49], is nonnegative with all row sums equal to either 1 or 0. A webpage that has no outlinks will have all 0's in its corresponding row of the matrix A. If one assumes that there are no such webpages in the instance of the Web to be modeled (this is obviously not true in reality), then the matrix A is, by definition, a *row stochastic matrix* so that the power iteration in equation (7.4) reflects a Markov chain [61, 63] or random walk on the graph defined by the link structure (inlinks and outlinks) of the Web (or Google's cached instance of the Web).

An *irreducible* Markov chain is one in which every state can be (ulti-mately) reached from all other states. In this context, we would say that there exists a path in the Web (or neighborhood) graph from node (or webpage) i to node j for all i, j. In addition, one can show [61, Ch. 8] that the stationary distribution vector $\vec{x}$ for such a Markov chain is unique and positive[7] — desirable properties for a PageRank vector. Several per-turbations are made to the stochastic matrix A to produce an irreducible Markov chain [49]. Figure 7.3 illustrates one candidate approach (origi-nally used by Google developers Brin and Page) to guarantee irreducibility.

---

[7]Based on the Perron–Frobenius theorem, this would be the dominant left eigenvector corresponding to the eigenvalue $\lambda = 1$.

As with the HITS example (Figure 7.2), consider the 5-node web graph from Figure 7.1 as a sample link structure for ranking webpages. From that directed graph the corresponding 5×5 transition probability matrix $A = [a_{ij}]$ is given by

$$A = \begin{pmatrix} 0 & 0 & 0.5 & 0 & 0.5 \\ 0.5 & 0 & 0.5 & 0 & 0 \\ 0 & 0.5 & 0 & 0.5 & 0 \\ 0.5 & 0 & 0 & 0 & 0.5 \\ 0 & 0 & 1 & 0 & 0 \end{pmatrix}.$$

Should it be known (perhaps from weblogs or data mining) that accesses to webpage (or node) 4 are twice as likely to be followed by an access to webpage 1, as opposed to webpage 5, then the fourth row of A could be redefined as

$$(\ .6667 \quad 0 \quad 0 \quad 0 \quad .3333\ )\ .$$

Such external information (to the link structure) can be exploited to better reflect actual usage patterns of the Web.

If $p = 0.85$ is the fraction of time that the random walk (or Markov chain) follows an outlink and $(1 - p) = 0.15$ is the fraction of time that an arbitrary webpage is chosen (independent of the link structure of the web graph), then the derived PageRank vector $\vec{x}$ or normalized left-hand eigenvector of the modified stochastic (Google) matrix

$$pA + (1 - p)E, \ \text{where } E = \vec{e}\vec{e}^T/5,$$

can be shown (with 4 significant decimal digits) to be

$$\vec{x}^T = (\ 0.1716 \quad 0.1666 \quad 0.3214 \quad 0.1666 \quad 0.1737\ )\ .$$

Here, $\vec{e}^T = (\ 1 \quad 1 \quad 1 \quad 1 \quad 1\ )$ and $\vec{x}_0^T = \vec{e}^T/5$. If the set of webpages judged relevant to a user's query is $\{1, 2, 3\}$, then webpage 3 would be ranked as the most relevant, followed by webpages 1 and 2, respectively.

Figure 7.3: PageRank example using the 5-node graph from Figure 7.1.

A rank-1 perturbation[8] of the $n \times n$ stochastic matrix A defined by

$$pA + (1 - p)E, \text{ where } E = \vec{e}\vec{e}^T/n,$$

models *random* surfing of the Web in that not all webpages are accessed via outlinks from other pages. This perturbation of the matrix A is referred to as the *Google* matrix [49]. The fraction of time an arbitrary webpage is selected (in the web graph) is given by $(1 - p)$. Hence, the fraction of time a webpage is visited following the link structure (via a random walk) is p. As the original matrix A reflects the *true* link structure of the Web, it is highly desirable to make minimal perturbations to force irreducibility.

7.2.2 PageRank Implementation

As mentioned in [63], PageRank is updated about once a month and does not require any analysis of the actual (semantic) content of the Web or of a user's queries. Google must find semantic matches (webpages) with a user's query first and then rank order the returned list according to PageRank. As mentioned earlier, the computation of PageRank is quite a challenge in and of itself. What can one do to make this computation tractable? As summarized in [49], approaches to compute PageRank via the power iteration

$$\vec{x}_j^T = \vec{x}_{j-1}^T[pA + (1 - p)E]$$

may involve (i) parallelization of the sparse vector-matrix multiplications, (ii) partitioning of the stochastic iteration matrix [50, 54] (e.g., into a block of webpages with outlinks and another block of those without outlinks), (iii) extrapolation or aggregation techniques [40, 41] to speed up convergence to the stationary distribution vector $\vec{x}$, and (iv) adaptive methods [39] which track the convergence of individual elements in $\vec{x}_j$.

Updating PageRank scores is another implementation concern. As the Web is certainly not static, how useful are the current scores for reflecting ongoing changes to the link structure? Research in the use of old PageRank scores to estimate new PageRank scores (without reconstructing the Markov chain) is ongoing [48, 23, 49]. Taking into account changes in the link structure (addition/deletion of inlinks and outlinks) must be addressed as well as the addition/deletion of webpages themselves. The latter issue can definitely affect the size of the stochastic iteration matrix A and its

---

[8]$\vec{e}$ is an n-vector of all ones.

perturbations — making a difficult computation even harder. Approximate methods for updating Markov chains [48, 49] are promising alternatives to the computationally intensive *exact* methods (see [23]). This problem alone should provide ample fodder for research in large-scale link-based search technologies.

7.2.3   PageRank Summary

Similar to HITS, PageRank can suffer from topic drift. The *importance* of a webpage (as defined by its query-independent PageRank score) does not necessarily reflect the *relevance* of the webpage to a user's query. Unpopular yet very relevant webpages may be missed with PageRank scoring. Some consider this a major weakness of Google [15]. On the other hand, the query independence of PageRank has made Google a great success in the speed and ease of web searching. A clear advantage of PageRank over the HITS approach lies in its resilience to spamming. Attempts to increase the number of inlinks to a webpage with hopes of increasing its PageRank are possible, but their global effects are limited. Some spam recognition techniques have been developed [81, 16]. On the other hand, as described in Section 7.1.2, the HITS algorithm can be greatly affected by changes to the neighborhood graph $\mathcal{N}$.

Chapter 8

User Interface Considerations

The concept of user interface, or creating the tool that people use to interact with the search engine, is an important part of the burgeoning field of *human–computer interaction* (HCI). The significance of the user interface cannot be emphasized enough, because often the user will judge the performance of the search engine not on the final results of the search as much as the perceived hoops the user has jumped through to get those results. For example, if it is difficult to type a search term in the small fill-in box, or there is uncertainty how the engine will handle the search terms or relevant results seem questionable, then there is a possibility of user dissatisfaction. It is certainly beyond the scope of this book to discuss all the related issues concerning user interfaces. The focus of *USE* is more on the specific aspects of developing an interface for a search engine. Ben Shneiderman and Catherine Plaisant's *Designing the User Interface: Strategies of Effective Human-Computer Interaction* provides an excellent review of the *broad* field of HCI along with a general framework for the design of interfaces. (Much of the material in this chapter references their work.) They define a well-designed user interactive system as one where "the interface almost disappears, enabling users to concentrate on their work exploration, or pleasure" [76].

8.1 General Guidelines

In general terms, interface designers are encouraged to develop guidelines and goals of what the interface should do, i.e., what tasks/subtasks must be carried out for the users. An interface for a general user with limited search skills may need to be much different from that for a skilled searcher. The skilled searcher prefers to understand how the search operates in order to narrow or broaden it and to ensure its thoroughness, whereas the novice merely wants *an answer*. In *Information Seeking in Electronic Environments*, Marchionini presents a broad view of the user–computer relationship [58]. He writes that systems should not only accommodate analytical, structured searchers, but he also sees the importance of more unstructured browsing (one of the early *advantages* of the Web), which can be considered a valuable type of learning method for many potential users. Moreover, the distinction between planned searching and simple browsing is often blurred. Therefore, says Marchionini, "A grand challenge for interface designers is to create new features that take advantage of the unique characteristics of each medium" [58].

One example of a searchable database that takes advantage of the browsing characteristics of the Web is the experimental Relation Attribute Viewer (RAVE) located at `http://squash.ils.unc.edu/rave/`. Designed by Marchionini's Interaction Design Laboratory at the University of North Carolina, RAVE has links to a host of different databases including the U.S. Department of Energy's Information Administration Browser++, which allows users to query and browse a website of 10,000 pages [59].

Interface building tools are in a continual state of evolution. They include tools such as grammars, menu-selection trees, and transition diagrams that can be used to define the specifications for the interface. Then there is a different set of development software for actually building the interface. Originally, computer programs written in languages such as Java, C, and C++ were used to build interfaces, but those have been replaced by more powerful and specific software tools that shorten the time for initial layouts and subsequent revisions. Shneiderman and Plaisant devote an entire chapter to software applications that can aid in overall interface design in *Designing the User Interface: Strategies of Effective Human-Computer Interaction* [76].

8.2   Search Engine Interfaces

Although having the right tools for building the interface between the search engine and user is important, equally critical is deciding how the search engine features will be manifested in the user interface. The underlying premise in all user interfaces is that ideally the interface must be designed to meet a user's needs. This creates problems in search engine interfaces because the range of expertise in search engine users varies from beginner to expert. Further complicating the interface design issues is that a user's information needs range from specific and related fact finding to browsing and exploration. (To browse and explore means the search engine must have the ability to do concept searching — one of the strengths of vector space modeling.) An interface must be able to handle both types of searches. Ideally, systems should initially be able to accommodate first time users, who as they gain experience with the system may require a much wider range of search tools for composing, saving, and revising queries.

Nielsen [65] is also in favor of keeping the search simple initially by avoiding Boolean search operators in the primary search interface. He is even in favor of using less friendly sounding links such as "Advanced Search" as a type of "intimidation" to keep inexperienced searchers from getting in over their heads too early.

8.2.1 Form Fill-in

Although early search mechanisms used a command line structure to make a query, that type of interaction style has fallen by the wayside. Currently, the predominant style is a simple form fill-in, where the user types a query into the designated blank line on the screen. This is a simple, logical, and easy task for the user to learn, which explains their popularity. However, sometimes the space is not large enough for more than just one or two words, which can keep the user from offering additonal terms that may be useful in the search [65].

Some consideration should also be given to the manner in which the user sends/invokes the query. For example, do you hit the enter key or press the search button? Can the user backspace or delete a misspelled word easily? Can the search engine do a spell check of the word?

Interestingly enough, if one looks at current commercial search engines (e.g., Google, Ask Jeeves, Yahoo!), there is a simple, usually one-line query form but a link to a more advanced search form. This advanced form may have drop-down menus that allow the user to fine tune the query for exact word matches, types of domains searched, etc. This advanced search requires more thought, time, and effort on the user's part — a reasonable trade-off.

NLQs, where the user has been encouraged to write out his or her query in the form of a question, have also been de-emphasized in the past few years. The general consensus has been that that they are slower to process the query, and NLQs somewhat mislead the user to think that computers are actually capable of understanding human language [65, 76].

8.2.2   Display Considerations

While there are numerous layouts and designs that will attract user attention, it is advisable that designers try to control themselves [76]. For example, limiting a display to three fonts and four colors is a recommended restraint. Also, keep in mind that a significant segment of users are color blind and have difficulty distinguishing red letters on a green background.

Experts in interface design tend to oppose the use of *anthropomorphism,* or assigning human traits to inanimate objects. Current literature indicates that while anthropomorphism may seem "cute" at first, it soon becomes irritating and a constant reminder that the user is working with a computer, which defeats the original purpose of anthropomorphism [76].

8.2.3   Progress Indication

A progress indicator or some temporary onscreen notification is a necessary feature. In other words, while the search is being conducted the user needs to know what the system is doing with the query. A "Please wait" prompt or some type of "countdown" visual to let the user know that the results are coming will suffice in this situation. Ironically, while it is important that results come quickly (e.g., within 2 to 5 seconds), there is a problem for the user if they come back *too fast,* i.e., instantaneously. This is easy to understand. For example, if the user types a search term and presses the return key and the engine comes back within a half second with "No results found," a degree of skepticism emerges whether the engine ever searched or accessed anything (see the shoe salesperson analogy below). In this instance, if the wait was only a second or two longer, the user would probably be satisfied that at least the search engine was executing properly.

Searching for Shoes

If you have ever worked as a shoe salesperson or waited tables for any length of time, you soon learn a valuable *trick* to keep the customer happy or at least avoid being hassled.

When a customer asks for a specific style and size of shoe or specific food item such as chocolate cheesecake that you know you are out of, the wise employee (rather than risk sounding brusque with a curt "We are out of that") will go the back room or kitchen and pretend to look anyway. Upon returning with the bad news, the customer is usually more understanding. After all, you gave it your best *search*.

The same is true with search engines. Come back instantaneously with "No results found" and you have a potentially dissatisfied user. Wait a few seconds and return the same message, and the user knows at least the search engine *tried*.

8.2.4   No Penalties for Error

If the user perceives that any command can be undone or cannot "hurt the system," he or she is more likely to be comfortable with the system. Along the same lines, Shneiderman and Plaisant [76] encourage designers if they use error messages to use ones that are not harsh. Instead of announcing "Syntax Error!!!" after an unrecognizable query has been rejected, perhaps a better alternative would be a message such as "Please add a pair of closing quotation marks to define your query."

8.2.5   Results

Search engine results or a user's ability to manipulate search engine results is one area where users seem to have accepted a standard that is less than what it should be. Thus far, the standard fare is having hundreds to thousands of results displayed in order of their relevance with the search terms highlighted in brief or piecemeal descriptions. However, there is room for improvement.

Nielsen recommends that developers can save a user's time by avoiding the display of search scores (percentages or icons) because it is a waste of the user's time to interpret. Nielsen would like to see such features as having the search engine "collapse" results from the same directory or domain into just one link and to be able to recognize a quality link (such as a FAQ link) [65]. In their recommendations for text search interfaces, Shneiderman and Plaisant advocate that the resulting list of items/documents should be able to be manipulated in terms of the number of results and the ability to change the order, whether it be alphabetically, chronologically, or in terms of relevancy. Opportunities for relevance feedback, the ability to save results and send them to colleagues or export results to other programs also merits consideration. The clustering of results by attribute value or topic is another possibility that designers should consider implementing. One of the newer search engines, Vivisimo (`http://vivisimo.com`), has already made improvements in the area of clustering [76].

Another facet of displaying the results is telling the user *how* the search engine processed the query [76]. Did the system interpret the user's query as the user intended? If so, was the user informed of this? For example, in advanced searches, users may use wildcards, quotations to mark phrases, or Boolean operators (see Chapter 5) such as *OR* and *AND* in their query. However, since there is a lack of standardization in search engines, each search engine may handle the query differently. It is important to indicate how the query was processed without confusing the user.

8.2.6　Test and Retest

The interface should be tested and retested by individuals who were not part of the original design team. This does not require dozens of individuals. Four or five users at the appropriate skill level, who are able to communicate their observations on a test version of an interface, will catch any egregious errors in design. Marchionini sees the advantage of continually studying and testing user interfaces. He also does not discount the importance of looking at patterns and strategies of novice users. In a way, they are the more natural users, and therefore the interfaces should be adapted to fit their predilections, instead of vice versa. Also, asking reference librarians who assist patrons daily could provide additional insights about searching patterns and user-friendly interfaces.

8.2.7 Final Considerations

Once all hard work has been done to build (and test) the best interface possible, designers should then take refuge in the philosophical words of encouragement from Marchionini, who in [58] reminds interface designers that maximum efficiency is not always agreeable to human nature. Although HCI's ultimate goal is to optimize performance, sometimes optimization may make tasks somewhat boring and impede performance. Marchionini maintains it is human nature to seek variety even at the expense of doing things at maximum efficiency. In other words, sometimes the best way to do something is the way the user prefers, not the designer.

Chapter 9

Further Reading

Many sources went into *USE*. Some of these sources deserve special mention not only because of their influence in our book but because they also provide additional and more complete understanding of specific topics surrounding search engines.

9.1   General Textbooks on IR

In our Data and Information Management course, which provided some of the impetus for writing this book, the textbook used was Gerald Kowalski's, *Information Retrieval Systems: Theory and Implementation* [45]. This general purpose book looks at many basic concepts of IR. It contains good examples of data structures, background material on indexing, and cataloging while covering important areas such as item normalization and clustering as it relates to generating a thesaurus. [45].

Another all-purpose book, *Information Storage and Retrieval* by Robert R. Korfhage [44], contains comprehensive chapters on query structures and document file preparation. In the "next iteration" of the Data and Information Management course taught in the spring of 1999, the Korfhage textbook was used. In contrast to the previously mentioned books, *Managing Gigabytes: Compressing and Indexing Documents and Images*, by I. H. Witten, A. Moffat, and T. C. Bell, is understandably more focused on storage issues, but it does address the subject of IR (indexing, queries, and index construction), albeit from a unique compression perspective.

One of the first books that covers various information retrieval topics was actually a collection of survey papers edited by William B. Frakes and Ricardo Baeza-Yates. Their 1992 book [30], *Information Retrieval: Data Structures & Algorithms*, contains several seminal works in this area, including the use of *signature-based* text retrieval methods by Christos Faloutsos and the development of ranking algorithms by Donna Harman. Ricardo Baeza-Yates and Berthier Ribeiro-Neto's [2] *Modern Information Retrieval* is another collection of well-integrated research articles from various authors with a computer-science perspective of information retrieval.

9.2   Computational Methods and Software

Two *SIAM Review* articles (Berry, Dumais, and O'Brien in 1995 [8] and Berry, Drmač, and Jessup in 1999 [7]) demonstrate the use of linear algebra for vector space IR models such as LSI. The latter of these articles [7] would be especially helpful to undergraduate students in applied mathematics or scientific computing. Details of matrix decompositions such as the QR factorization and SVD are found in the popular reference book [33], *Matrix Computations*, by Gene Golub and Charles Van Loan. The work of Kolda and O'Leary [43] demonstrates the use of alternative decompositions such as the SDD for vector space IR models. Recent work by Simon and Zha [77] on updating LSI models demonstrates how to maintain accurate low-rank approximations to term-by-document matrices in the context of dynamic text collections. Berry and Fierro in [12] discuss updating LSI in the context of the ULV (or URV) matrix decomposition.

In order to compute the SVD of large sparse term-by-document matrices, iterative methods such as Arnoldi [56], Lanczos [47, 67], subspace iteration [70, 67], and trace minimization [74] can be used. In [10], Berry discusses how the last three methods are implemented within the software libraries SVDPACK (Fortran 77) [5] and SVDPACKC (ANSI C) [6], which are available in the public domain.

Simple descriptions with MATLAB examples for Lanczos-based methods are available in [3], and a good survey of public-domain software for Lanczos-type methods is available in [11]. Whereas most of the iterative methods used for computing the SVD are serial in nature, an interesting asynchronous technique for computing several of the largest singular triplets of a sparse matrix on a network of workstations is described in [84].

The work of Lehoucq [55] and Lehoucq and Sorensen [56] on the Arnoldi method should be considered for computing the SVD of sparse matrices. Their software is available in ARPACK [55]. If one ignores sparsity altogether or must compute the (truncated) SVD of relatively dense matrices, the LAPACK [1] and ScaLAPACK [17] software libraries are available. A quick summary of available software packages mentioned above along with their corresponding websites is provided in Table 9.1. The LSI website listed in Table 9.1 allows the user to search a few sample text collections using

Table 9.1: Useful websites for software and algorithm descriptions.

URL	*Description*
http://www.cs.utk.edu/~lsi	LSI website (papers, sample text collections, and client-servers for demonstrations)
http://www.netlib.org/svdpack	SVDPACK (Fortran-77) and SVDPACKC (ANSI C) libraries [5, 6]
http://www.netlib.org/templates	Postscript and HTML forms of [3] along with Fortran, C++, and MATLAB software
http://www.netlib.org/lapack	Latest Users' Guide [1] and Fortran 77, C, C++ software
http://www.netlib.org/scalapack	Latest ScaLAPACK User's Guide [17] and software and Parallel ARPACK (PARPACK) software
http://www.netlib.org/scalapack/ arpack96.tgz	Implicitly Restarted Arnoldi software in Fortran-77 [55]

LSI. Some of the client–server designs used in recent LSI implementations are discussed in [57].

With respect to link-structure algorithms, Langville and Meyer's detailed survey of eigenvector methods [49] along with Kumar, Raghavan, and Rajagopalan's [46] overview of the social aspects of the Web are most insightful. Langville and Meyer have also cowritten a more comprehensive book on search engine rankings for search engines (Google, Teoma) that utilize link-structure algorithms [51].

Moreover, in the past few years, SIAM's annual data mining conferences have included papers on the use of applied mathematics in search engines as well as in text and data mining. For more information, visit `www.siam.org/meetings`.

9.3   Search Engines

One of the toughest tasks in writing about this subject is staying current on commercial search engines. What we wrote today is not necessarily going to be true next week, so we recommend the on-line resource Search Engine Watch, edited by Danny Sullivan. Search Engine Watch tracks the major search engines, their latest features, and how to better utilize them both as a user and a webmaster. For a fee, subscribers can access additional information and receive electronic updates. Another site which has the librarian-professional searcher perspective is the electronic newsletter *Sitelines.* Sponsored by Workingfaster.com, a training company for power searchers, *Sitelines* has weblog-type articles from correspondents and evaluative commentary from editor Rita Vine. For more information on Search Engine Watch and *Sitelines*, see Table 9.2.

9.4   User Interfaces

Ben Shneiderman and Catherine Plaisant's book *Designing the User Interface: Strategies of Effective Human-Computer Interaction* [76] is more than a summary of the state of HCI. The book, now in its fourth edition, has a kind of renaissance quality about it. Shneiderman and Plaisant are not content to just write specifically about computer interfaces but take a broad, widespread approach covering topics ranging from interface models to specific design guidelines that makes the book more enjoyable and relevant.

Table 9.2: Useful websites for current search engine evaluation and user interface designs.

URL	*Description*
`http://www.searchenginewatch.com`	Current information on commercial search engines
`http://www.workingfaster.com/` `sitelines`	A newsletter for professional searchers that looks at web search tools
`http://squash.ils.unc.edu`	Interaction Design Lab (Gary Marchionini)
`http://bailando.sims.berkeley.edu/` `flamenco.html`	The FLAMENCO Search Interface Project, which incorporates metadata into search interfaces

A similar book is Gary Marchionini's *Information Seeking in Electronic Environments* [58]. Marchionini's approach identifies users' information seeking patterns and then tries to match them to current information retrieval technologies. For a look at Marchionini's later efforts see the website listed in Table 9.2. Also, Ricardo Baeza-Yates and Berthier Ribeiro-Neto's [2] *Modern Information Retrieval* has a lengthy chapter dedicated to user interfaces and visualization written by Marti Hearst.

Bibliography

[1] E. ANDERSON, Z. BAI, C. BISCHOF, J. DEMMEL, J. DONGARRA, J. D. CRUZ, A. GREENBAUM, S. HAMMARLING, A. MCKENNEY, S. OSTROUCHOV, AND D. SORENSEN, *LAPACK Users' Guide*, second ed., SIAM, Philadelphia, 1995.

[2] R. BAEZA-YATES AND B. RIBEIRO-NETO, *Modern Information Retrieval*, Addison–Wesley, Reading, MA, 1999.

[3] R. BARRETT, M. W. BERRY, T. F. CHAN, J. DEMMEL, J. DONATO, J. DONGARRA, V. EIJKHOUT, R. POZO, C. ROMINE, AND H. VAN DER VORST, *Templates for the Solution of Linear Systems: Building Blocks for Iterative Methods*, SIAM, Philadelphia, 1993.

[4] D. BERG, *A Guide to the Oxford English Dictionary*, Oxford University Press, Oxford, 1993.

[5] M. BERRY, *SVDPACK: A Fortran 77 Software Library for the Sparse Singular Value Decomposition*, Tech. Report CS–92–159, University of Tennessee, Knoxville, TN, June 1992.

[6] M. BERRY, T. DO, G. O'BRIEN, V. KRISHNA, AND S. VARADHAN, *SVDPACKC: Version 1.0 User's Guide*, Tech. Report CS–93–194, University of Tennessee, Knoxville, TN, October 1993.

[7] M. W. BERRY, Z. DRMAČ, AND E. R. JESSUP, *Matrices, vector spaces, and information retrieval*, SIAM Review, 41 (1999), pp. 335–362.

[8] M. W. BERRY, S. T. DUMAIS, AND G. W. O'BRIEN, *Using linear algebra for intelligent information retrieval*, SIAM Review, 37 (1995), pp. 573–595.

[9] M. BERRY, B. HENDRICKSON, AND P. RAGHAVAN, *Sparse matrix reordering schemes for browsing hypertext*, in Lectures in Applied Mathematics Vol. 32: The Mathematics of Numerical Analysis, J. Renegar, M. Shub, and S. Smale, eds., American Mathematical Society, Providence, RI, 1996, pp. 99–123.

[10] M. W. BERRY, *Large scale singular value computations*, International Journal of Supercomputer Applications, 6 (1992), pp. 13–49.

[11] M. W. BERRY, *Survey of public-domain Lanczos-based software*, in Proceedings of the Cornelius Lanczos Centenary Conference, J. Brown, M. Chu, D. Ellison, and R. Plemmons, eds., SIAM, Philadelphia, 1997, pp. 332–334.

[12] M. W. BERRY AND R. D. FIERRO, *Low-rank orthogonal decompositions for information retrieval applications*, Numerical Linear Algebra with Applications, 3 (1996), pp. 301–328.

[13] K. BHARAT AND A. BRODER, *Estimating the relative size and overlap of public web search engines*, in 7th International World Wide Web Conference, Paper FP37, Elsevier Science, New York, 1998.

[14] K. BHARAT AND M. HENZINGER, *Improved algorithms for topic distillation in hyperlinked environments*, in Proceedings of the Twenty-First International ACM SIGIR Conference on Research and Development in Information Retrieval, ACM Press, New York, 1998, pp. 104–111.

[15] K. BHARAT AND G. MIHAILIA, *When experts agree: Using non-affilated experts to rank popular topics*, ACM Transactions on Information Systems, 20 (2002), pp. 47–58.

[16] M. BIANCHINI, M. GORI, AND F. SCARSELLI, *Inside PageRank*, ACM Transactions on Internet Technology, 4 (2004). In press.

[17] L. S. BLACKFORD, J. CHOI, A. CLEARY, E. D'AZEVEDO, J. DEMMEL, I. DHILLON, J. DONGARRA, S. HAMMARLING, G. HENRY, A. PETITET, K. STANLEY, D. WALKER, AND R. C. WHALEY, *ScaLAPACK Users' Guide*, first ed., SIAM, Philadelphia, 1997.

[18] A. BOOKSTEIN, *On the perils of merging Boolean and weighted retrieval systems*, Journal of the American Society for Information Science, 29 (1978), pp. 156–158.

[19] A. BOOKSTEIN, *Probability and fuzzy set applications to information retrieval*, Annual Review of Information Science and Technology, 20 (1985), pp. 117–152.

[20] S. BRIN AND L. PAGE, *The anatomy of a large-scale hypertextual web search engine*, in Proceedings of the Seventh International Conference on the World Wide Web 7 (WWW7), Elsevier Science, Amsterdam, 1998, pp. 107–117.

[21] S. BRIN, L. PAGE, R. MOTWAMI, AND T. WINOGRAD, *The PageRank Citation Ranking: Bringing Order to the Web*, Tech. Report, Stanford Digital Library Technologies Project, Stanford, CA, 1998.

[22] C. BUCKLEY, A. SINGHAL, M. MITRA, AND G. SALTON, *New retrieval approaches using SMART: TREC 4*, in Proceedings of the Fourth Text Retrieval Conference (TREC-4), D. Harman, ed., Gaithersburg, MD, 1996, Department of Commerce, National Institute of Standards and Technology. NIST Special Publication 500-236.

[23] S. CHIEN, C. DWORK, R. KUMAR, D. SIMON, AND D. SIVAKUMAR, *Link evolution: Analysis and algorithms*, in Proceedings of the Workshop on Algorithms and Models for the Web Graph, Vancouver, BC, Canada, 2002.

[24] C. CLEVERDON, *Optimizing convenient online access to bibliographic databases*, in Document Retrieval Systems, P. Willett, ed., Taylor Graham, London, 1988, pp. 32–41.

[25] S. DEERWESTER, S. DUMAIS, G. FURNAS, T. LANDAUER, AND R. HARSHMAN, *Indexing by latent semantic analysis*, Journal of the American Society for Information Science, 41 (1990), pp. 391–407.

[26] I. DUFF, R. GRIMES, AND J. LEWIS, *Sparse matrix test problems*, ACM Transactions on Mathematical Software, 15 (1989), pp. 1–14.

[27] S. T. DUMAIS, *Improving the retrieval of information from external sources*, Behavior Research Methods, Instruments, & Computers, 23 (1991), pp. 229–236.

[28] C. ECKART AND G. YOUNG, *The approximation of one matrix by another of lower rank*, Psychometrika, 1 (1936), pp. 211–218.

[29] C. FALOUTSOS, *Signature files*, in Information Retrieval: Data Structures & Algorithms, W. B. Frakes and R. Baeza-Yates, eds., Prentice–Hall, Englewood Cliffs, NJ, 1992, pp. 44–65.

[30] W. B. FRAKES AND R. BAEZA-YATES, *Information Retrieval: Data Structures & Algorithms*, Prentice–Hall, Englewood Cliffs, NJ, 1992.

[31] R. FUNG AND B. D. FAVERO, *Applying Bayesian networks to information retrieval*, Communications of the ACM, 58 (1995), pp. 27–30.

[32] F. GEY, *Inferring probability of relevance using the method of logistic regression*, in Proceedings of the Seventeenth Annual ACM-SIGIR Conference, W. B. Croft and C. van Rijsbergen, eds., Dublin, Ireland, 1994, Springer-Verlag, New York, 1994, pp. 222–241.

[33] G. GOLUB AND C. V. LOAN, *Matrix Computations*, third ed., The Johns Hopkins University Press, Baltimore, MD, 1996.

[34] D. HARMAN, *Ranking algorithms*, in Information Retrieval: Data Structures & Algorithms, W. B. Frakes and R. Baeza-Yates, eds., Prentice–Hall, Englewood Cliffs, NJ, 1992, pp. 363–392.

[35] D. HARMAN, ED., *Proceedings of the Third Text Retrieval Conference (TREC-3)*, Gaithersburg, MD, 1995, Department of Commerce, National Institute of Standards and Technology. NIST Special Publication 500-225.

[36] D. HARMAN, *Relevance feedback revisited*, in Proceedings of the Fifteenth Annual International ACM SIGIR Conference on Research and Development in Information Retrieval, Copenhagen, Denmark, June 21–24, 1992, pp. 1–10.

[37] S. JOHNSON, *The (evil) genius of content spammers*, Wired, 12.03 (2004).

[38] W. JONES AND G. FURNAS, *Pictures of relevance: A geometric analysis of similarity measures*, Journal of the American Society for Information Science, 38 (1987), pp. 420–442.

[39] S. KAMVAR, T. HAVELIWALA, AND G. GOLUB, *Adaptive Methods for the Computational of PageRank*, Tech. Report, Stanford University, Stanford, CA, 2003.

[40] S. KAMVAR, T. HAVELIWALA, C. MANNING, AND G. GOLUB, *Exploiting the Block Structure of the Web for Computing PageRank*, Tech. Report, Stanford University, Stanford, CA, 2003.

[41] S. KAMVAR, T. HAVELIWALA, C. MANNING, AND G. GOLUB, *Extrapolation methods for accelerating PageRank computations*, in Proceedings of the Twelfth International Conference on the World Wide Web 12 (WWW12), Budapest, Hungary, 2003, ACM Press, New York, 2003, pp. 261–270.

[42] D. KARR, *The search engine wars*, NPR Morning Edition (Apr. 16, 2004). http://www.npr.org/programs/morning/features/2004/apr/google, accessed August 24, 2004.

[43] T. G. KOLDA AND D. P. O'LEARY, *A semidiscrete matrix decomposition for latent semantic indexing in information retrieval*, ACM Transactions on Information Systems, 16 (1998), pp. 322–346.

[44] R. R. KORFHAGE, *Information Storage and Retrieval*, John Wiley & Sons, Inc., New York, 1997.

[45] G. KOWALSKI, *Information Retrieval Systems: Theory and Implementation*, Kluwer Academic Publishers, Boston, MA, 1997.

[46] R. KUMAR, P. RAGHAVAN, AND S. RAJAGOPALAN, *The Web and social networks*, IEEE Computer, 35 (2002), pp. 32–36.

[47] C. LANCZOS, *An iteration method for the solution of the eigenvalue problem of linear differential and integral operators*, Journal of Research of the National Bureau of Standards, 45 (1950), pp. 255–282.

[48] A. LANGVILLE AND C. MEYER, *Updating the Stationary Vector of an Irreducible Markov Chain*, Tech. Report CRSC02-TR33, North Carolina State University, Raleigh, NC, 2002.

[49] A. N. LANGVILLE AND C. D. MEYER, *A survey of eigenvector methods for Web information retrieval*, SIAM Review, 47 (2005), pp. 135–161.

[50] A. LANGVILLE AND C. MEYER, *Deeper inside PageRank*, Internet Mathematics, 1 (2003), pp. 335–380.

[51] A. LANGVILLE AND C. MEYER, *Understanding Search Engine Rankings: Google's PageRank, Teoma's HITS, and Other Ranking Algorithms*, Princeton University Press, Princeton, NJ, 2005. In press.

[52] R. R. LARSON, *Evaluation of advanced retrieval techniques in an experimental online catalog*, Journal of the American Society for Information Science, 43 (1992), pp. 34–53.

[53] S. LAWRENCE AND C. L. GILES, *Searching the world wide web*, Science, 280 (1998), pp. 98–100.

[54] C. LEE, G. GOLUB, AND S. ZENIOS, *Partial State Space Aggregation Based on Lumpability and its Application to PageRank*, Tech. Report, Stanford University, Stanford, CA, 2003.

[55] R. B. LEHOUCQ, *Analysis and Implementation of an Implicitly Restarted Arnoldi Iteration*, Ph.D. thesis, Rice University, Houston, TX, 1995.

[56] R. B. LEHOUCQ AND D. C. SORENSEN, *Deflation techniques for an implicitly restarted Arnoldi iteration*, SIAM Journal on Matrix Analysis and Applications, 17 (1996), pp. 789–821.

[57] T. A. LETSCHE AND M. W. BERRY, *Large-scale information retrieval with latent semantic indexing*, Information Sciences, 100 (1997), pp. 105–137.

[58] G. MARCHIONINI, *Information Seeking in Electronic Environments*, Cambridge University Press, New York, 1995.

[59] G. MARCHIONINI, *From information retrieval to information interaction*, in Proceedings of the European Conference on Information Retrieval, 2004. Keynote address is available on-line at http://ils.unc.edu/~march/ECIR.pdf, accessed August 1, 2004.

[60] THE MATHWORKS INC., *Using MATLAB*, Natick, MA, 1998. Version 5.

[61] C. D. MEYER, *Matrix Analysis and Applied Linear Algebra*, SIAM, Philadelphia, 2000.

[62] L. MIRSKY, *Symmetric gauge functions and unitarily invariant norms*, The Quarterly Journal of Mathematics, 11 (1960), pp. 50–59.

[63] C. MOLER, *The World's Largest Matrix Computation.* MATLAB News & Notes, The MathWorks, October 2002.

[64] NATIONAL LIBRARY OF MEDICINE, *UMLS* 2002 *Metathesaurus*, 2002. http://www.nlm.nih.gov/research/umls/archive/2002AA/META2. HTML, accessed March 19, 2004.

[65] J. NIELSEN, *Designing Web Usability*, New Riders Publishing, Indianapolis, IN, 2000.

[66] G. O'BRIEN, *Information Management Tools for Updating an SVD-Encoded Indexing Scheme*, Master's thesis, University of Tennessee, Knoxville, TN, 1994.

[67] B. PARLETT, *The Symmetric Eigenvalue Problem*, Prentice–Hall, Englewood Cliffs, NJ, 1980.

[68] J. POKORNÝ, *Web searching and information retrieval*, Computing in Science and Engineering, 6 (2004), pp. 43–47.

[69] D. RAGGETT, A. L. HORS, AND I. JACOBS, *Notes on Helping Search Engines Index Your Web Site*, Tech. Report, W3C, December 1999. http://www.w3.org/TR/html4/cover.html, accessed August 1, 2004.

[70] H. RUTISHAUSER, *Simultaneous iteration method for symmetric matrices*, Numerische Mathematik, 16 (1970), pp. 205–223.

[71] G. SALTON AND C. BUCKLEY, *Term weighting approaches in automatic text retrieval*, Information Processing and Management, 24 (1988), pp. 513–523.

[72] G. SALTON AND C. BUCKLEY, *Improving retrieval performance by relevance feedback*, Journal of the American Society for Information Science, 41 (1990), pp. 288–297.

[73] G. SALTON AND M. MCGILL, *Introduction to Modern Information Retrieval*, McGraw–Hill, New York, 1983.

[74] A. H. SAMEH AND J. A. WISNIEWSKI, *A trace minimization algorithm for the generalized eigenvalue problem*, SIAM Journal on Numerical Analysis, 19 (1982), pp. 1243–1259.

[75] J. SHERMAN, *Yahoo! birth of a new machine*, Searchenginewatch (2004). http://www.searchenginewatch.com, accessed February 18, 2004.

[76] B. SHNEIDERMAN AND C. PLAISANT, *Designing the User Interface: Strategies of Effective Human-Computer Interaction*, fourth ed., Addison–Wesley, Boston, MA, 2004.

[77] H. SIMON AND H. ZHA, *On Updating Problems in Latent Semantic Indexing*, Tech. Report CSE-97-011, The Pennsylvania State University, State College, PA, 1997.

[78] A. SINGHAL, G. SALTON, M. MITRA, AND C. BUCKLEY, *Document Length Normalization*, Tech. Report TR95-1529, Cornell University, Department of Computer Science, Ithaca, NY, 1995.

[79] K. SPARCK JONES, *A statistical interpretation of term specificity and its applications in retrieval*, Journal of Documentation, 28 (1972), pp. 11–21.

[80] D. SULLIVAN, *How to use html meta tags*, Search Engine Watch (2002). http://www.searchenginewatch.com, accessed August 1, 2004.

[81] A. TSOI, G. MORINI, F. SCARSELLI, M. HAGENBUCHNER, AND M. MAGGINI, *Adaptive ranking of web pages*, in Proceedings of the Twelfth International Conference on the World Wide Web 12 (WWW12), ACM Press, New York, 2003, pp. 356–365.

[82] R. TYNER, *Sink or Swim: Internet Search Tools & Techniques*. Version 3.0, http://www.ouc.bc.ca/libr/connect96/search.html, accessed July 2, 2004.

[83] C. VAN RIJSBERGEN, *Information Retrieval*, second ed., Butterworths, London, 1979.

[84] S. VARADHAN, M. W. BERRY, AND G. H. GOLUB, *Approximating dominant singular triplets of large sparse matrices via modified moments*, Numerical Algorithms, 13 (1996), pp. 123–152.

[85] R. VINE, *Coming Soon - the Death of Search Engines?*, 2004. http://www.llrx.com/features/deathsearchengine.html, accessed July 24, 2004.

[86] I. H. WITTEN, A. MOFFAT, AND T. C. BELL, *Managing Gigabytes: Compressing and Indexing Documents and Images*, Van Nostrand Reinhold, New York, 1994.

[87] R. S. WURMAN, *Information Architects*, Graphis Press Corporation, Zurich, 1996.

[88] X. ZHANG, M. BERRY, AND P. RAGHAVAN, *Level search schemes for information and filtering*, Information Processing and Management, 37 (2001), pp. 313–334.

Index